MEL BAY'S GETTIN' TO..... FUNK GUITAR

1 2 3 4 5 6 7 8 9 0

Visit us on the Web at www.melbay.com — E-mail us at email@melbay.com

NOTES ABOUT THE AUTHOR

Ronald Muldrow received his B.M. in Jazz Studies from Roosevelt University and a M.M. in Studio/Jazz Guitar from the University of Southern California.

He has toured and recorded with Eddie Harris, Dr. Dre, The Staple Singers, Lou Rawls, Ronnie Laws, Booker T. Jones and Maceo Parker. He currently teaches at Cal Poly Pomona, CA

☆☆

ACKNOWLEDGEMENTS

I would like to thank Miller Pertum, A. Scott Galloway, Tom Johnson (Coda Music)

This book is dedicated to my mother Georgia Muldrow.

☆☆

CD CONTENTS

1 Rhythm only .... [1:14]
2 Guitar .... [0:24]
3 Rhythm only .... [0:24]
4 Guitar .... [0:24]
5 Guitar .... [0:22]
6 Rhythm only .... [0:14]
7 Guitar .... [0:21]
8 Rhythm only .... [0:18]
9 Guitar .... [0:22]
10 Rhythm only .... [0:21]
11 Guitar .... [0:21]
12 Rhythm only .... [0:24]
13 Guitar .... [0:24]
14 Rhythm only .... [0:23]
15 Guitar .... [0:21]
16 Rhythm only .... [0:23]
17 Guitar .... [0:22]
18 Rhythm only .... [0:23]
19 Guitar .... [0:22]
20 Rhythm only .... [0:18]
21 Rhythm only .... [0:42]
22 Rhythm only .... [0:40]
23 Rhythm only .... [0:36]
24 Rhythm only .... [0:40]
25 Rhythm only .... [0:37]
26 Rhythm only .... [0:46]
27 Rhythm only .... [0:43]
28 Guitar .... [0:16]
29 Guitar .... [0:16]
30 Guitar .... [0:16]
31 Guitar .... [0:16]
32 Guitar .... [0:16]
33 Guitar .... [0:16]
34 Guitar .... [0:26]
35 Guitar .... [0:26]
36 Guitar .... [0:26]
37 Guitar .... [0:26]
38 Guitar Etude 1 .... [0:26]
39 Guitar Etude 2 .... [0:29]
40 Guitar Etude 3 .... [0:26]
41 Guitar Etude 4 .... [0:25]
42 Guitar Etude 5 .... [0:26]
43 Guitar Etude 6 .... [0:26]
44 Guitar Etude 7 .... [0:26]
45 Guitar Etude 8 .... [0:26]
46 Guitar Etude 9 .... [0:26]
47 Guitar Etude 10 ..... [0:27]
48 Guitar Etude 11 ..... [0:30]
49 Guitar Etude 12 ..... [0:26]
50 Guitar Etude 13 ..... [0:26]
51 Guitar Etude 14 ..... [0:22]
52 Guitar Etude 15 ..... [0:26]
53 Guitar Etude 16 ..... [0:26]
54 Guitar Etude 17 ..... [0:26]
55 Guitar Etude 18 ..... [0:20]
56 Guitar Etude 19 ..... [0:20]
57 Guitar Etude 20 ..... [0:27]
58 Guitar Etude 21 ..... [0:21]
59 Guitar Etude 22 ..... [0:22]
60 Guitar Etude 23 ..... [0:27]
61 Guitar Etude 24 ..... [0:25]
62 Guitar Etude 25 ..... [0:25]
63 Guitar Etude 26 ..... [0:25]
64 Guitar Etude 27 ..... [0:26]
65 Guitar Etude 28 ..... [0:24]

Contents

☆☆

GETTING INTO FUNK

☆☆

This book deals with another part of the musical diaspora that makes up the American musical landscape, Funk. Funk can be used as a noun, verb, adjective or adverb. But the underlying musical issue is conceptual. No matter your level and/or genre of musical experience, we will look at the specific concept of Funk. When African and European aesthetics were mixed a unique music resulted-American music. How much of this mix is African or European somewhat defines America itself. Utilitarian music (i.e. music you can dance to) has a heavy dose of African aesthetics in the mixture. Funk is one of these genres. For the musician to eternalize this musical functionality she or he must understand funk is primarily music you listen to while one dances. The harmonic and melodic content can be extremely static and/or repetitive; everything is for the groove (beat).

The transition from jazz to R&B was led by groups like Louis Jordan in the late 40's and early 50's taking blues and tin pan alley standards used in jazz, but keeping them danceable, contrary to their be-bop contemporaries. The success of bands like Jordan's opened doors for others to come and focus on R&B (rhythm and blues). This eventually led to the development of different styles of R&B; "Soul music" and "Funk."

The creative genius of James Brown gave us the funk beginning with "Out of Sight," "I Got You," and "Papa's Got A Brand New Bag" and then consummated in "Cold Sweat." Brown, a dancer, vocalist as well as a multi-instrumentalist put the funk music together like a rhythmic puzzle, personally giving his band members their individual parts either by playing it on their instrument or singing it to them. The incredible focus in the early stages of funk music for all practical purposes was created single-handedly by Mr. Brown. This funk music Mr. Brown created focused on the beat.

The guitar is one of the primary instruments in funk music of the 60's and 70's. This popularity opened this market to unprecedented guitar sales and lead to a wave of effects the wah-wah pedal being the most popular along with distortion, phase and vibrato. The melodic and harmonic simplicity made the textural changes these effects provide a somewhat natural transition in the scheme of funk music. But after electric bassist Bootsy Collins left James Brown and the Flames he collaborated with George Clinton to make funk a viable genre of R&B as well as a way of life.

-Ronald Muldrow-

☆☆

Glossary Of Terms

Barline - 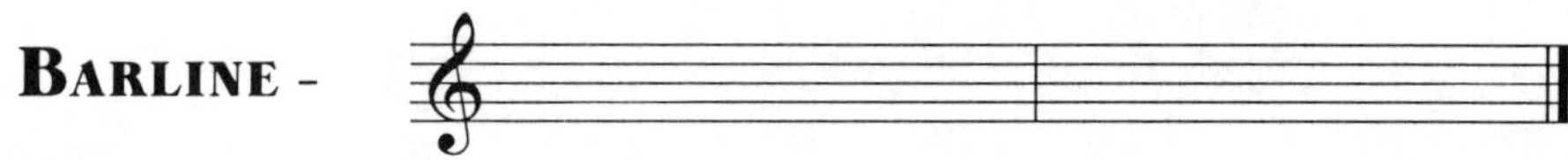

Chord - A minimum of three different pitches sounding simultaneously or functioning as such.

Dampening (Muting) - To touch a string or strings in a way that keep them from vibrating fully.

Glissando (Slide) ~~~ - To slide down or up a series of adjacent notes.

Interval - The distance between two or more pitches. Two pitches sounding simultneously or functioning as such.

Key - Adherence to the note-material of one of the major or minor scales.

Ledger Lines - Short lines added below or above the staff to accomodate notes ranging below or above the staff.

Measure or Bar - A unit of musical time consisting of a fixed number of note values.

Pitch - The perceived vibrations per second.

Rest - Musical silence.

Rhythm - Everything pertaining to the time aspect of music.

Root - The notes a chord originate from.

Syncopation - The accenting of weak instead of strong beats.

Triad - A chord consisting of three different notes.

Funk Terms

Terms Used When the Music Is Very Danceable - "Pocket," "In the pocket," "In the groove," "Killin'," "On the one," "Funky," "Nasty," "Ignorant," "Dumb," "In the cut," "I'm feelin' it," "Lockin'."

Fatback - Accent on two and four.

Chicken Scratchin', Chinkin' - The constant eighth or sixteenth note usually chordal rhythmic pattern.

Bottom - Usually refers to the bass pattern.

☆☆

NOTE VALUES

WHOLE	HALF	QUARTER	EIGHTH	SIXTEENTH

One whole note is equal to two half notes.

One half note is equal to two quarter notes.

One quarter note equals two eighth notes.

One eighth note is equal to two sixteenth notes.

RESTS

A rest(s) is the notated pause(s) within a musical space.

WHOLE	HALF	QUARTER	EIGHTH	SIXTEENTH

Tied Notes

Dotted Notes

Dots add half of the original note value to the original note.

Triplets

A quarter note triplet equals one half note.

An eighth note triplet equals one quarter note.

☆☆

Scales

Chromatic Scale

A half step is the shortest interval between two notes. A chromatic scale has all half steps. A whole tone scale has all whole steps. Other scales have a mix of both.

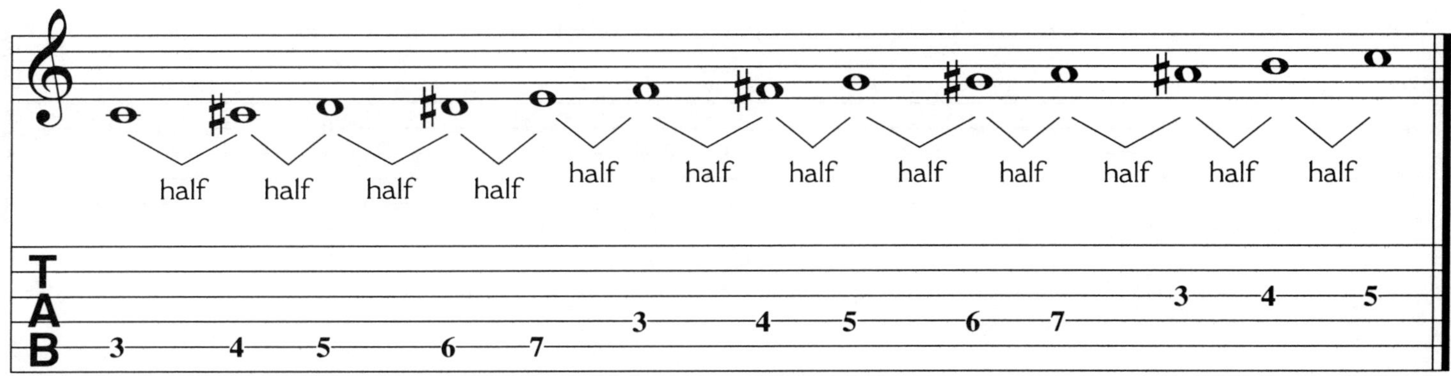

Whole Tone Scale

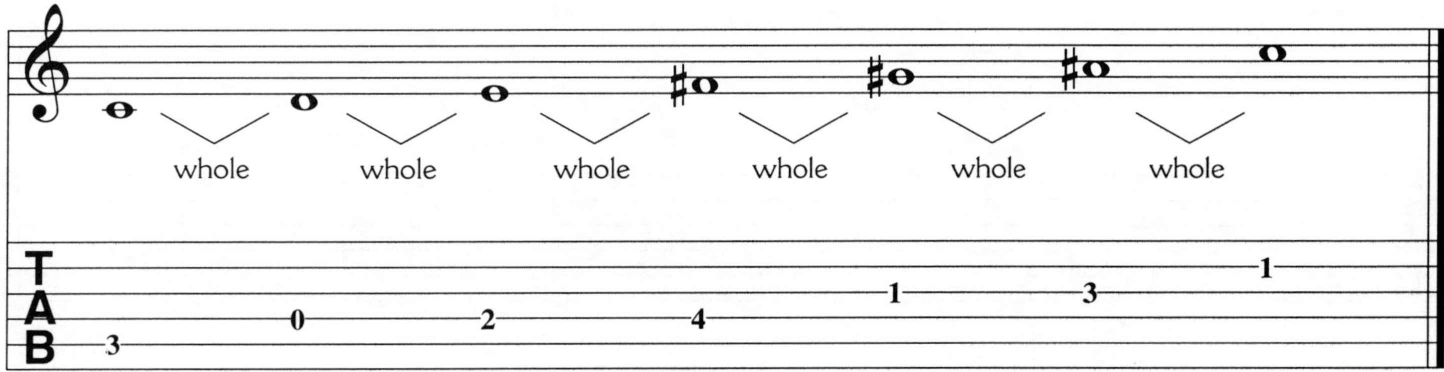

Diatonic (Major) Scale

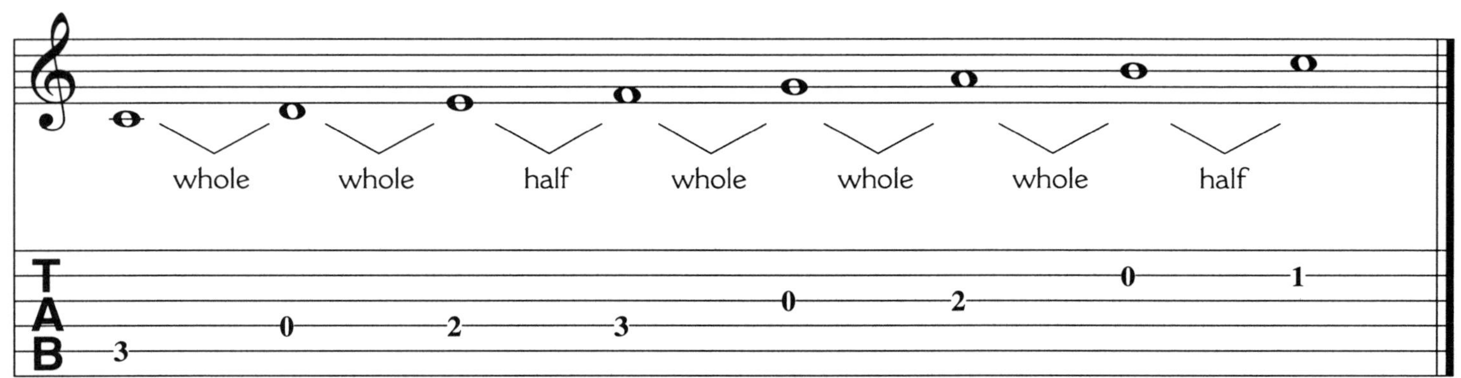

Blues Scale

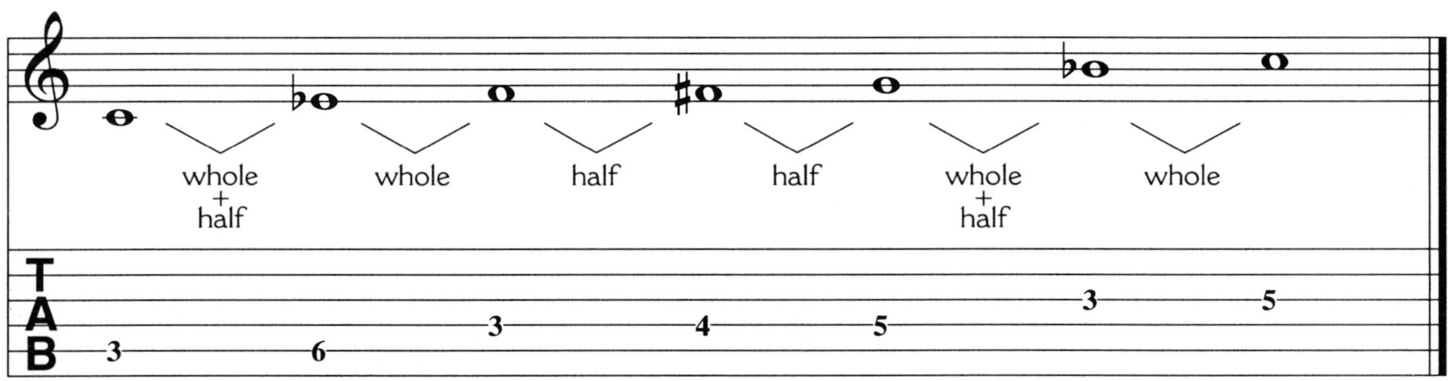

Major Scales

C

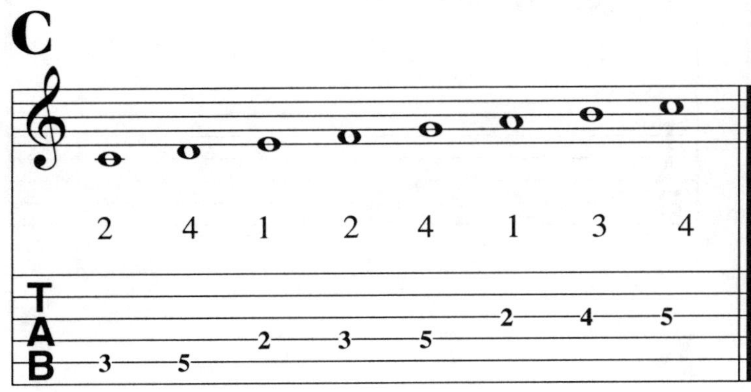

D♭

D

E♭

E

F

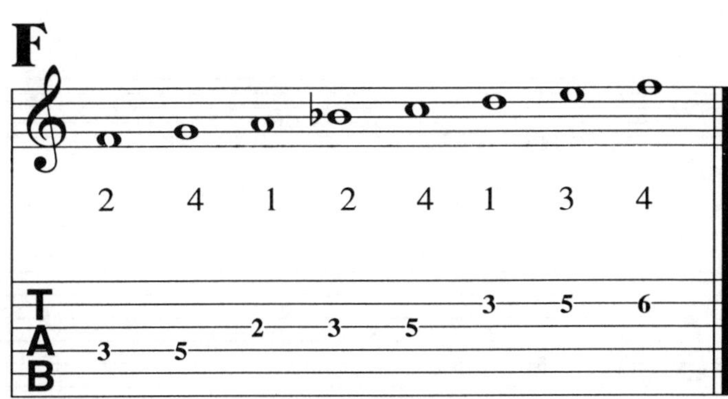

G♭

G

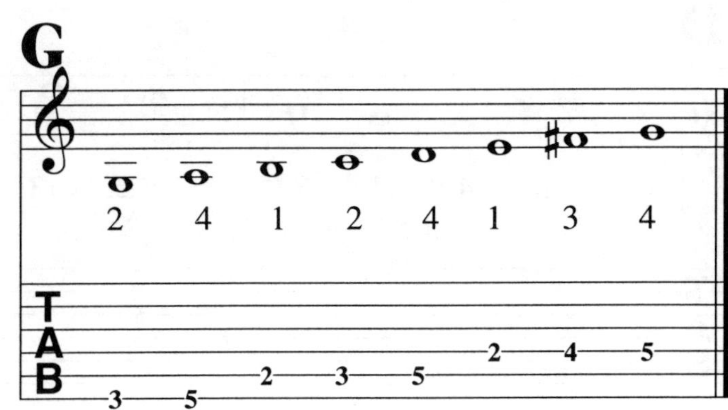

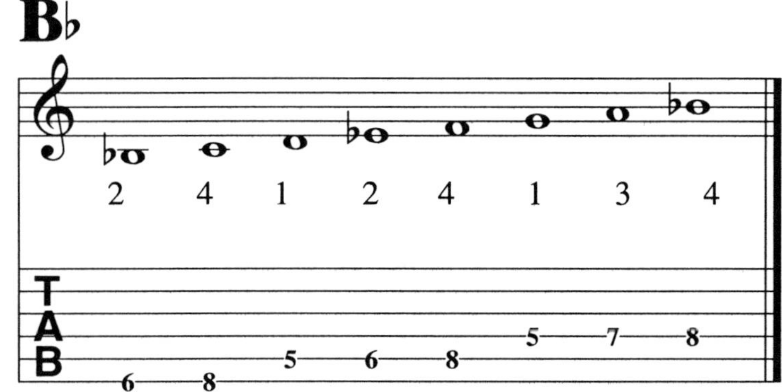

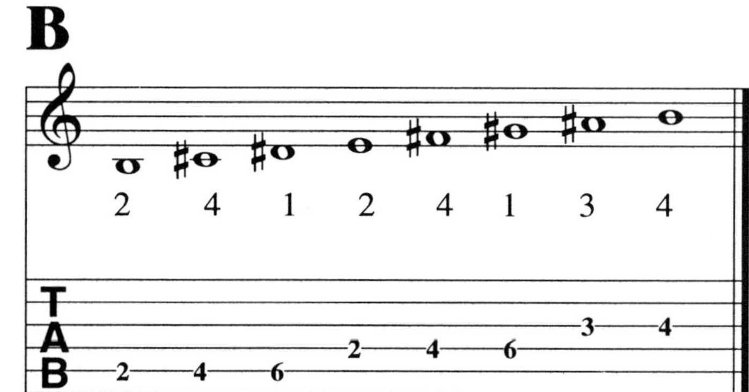

Harmonic Minor Scales

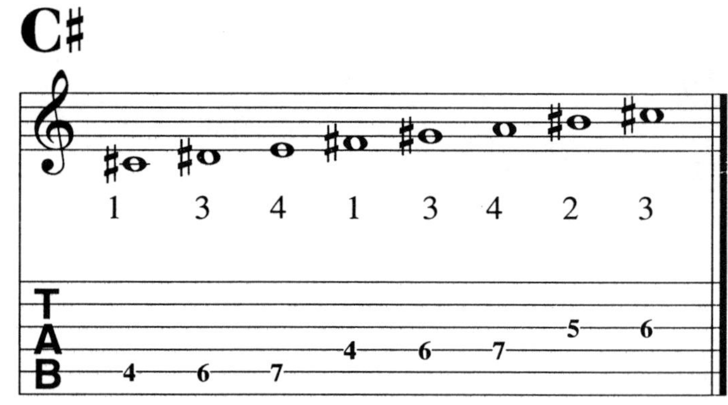

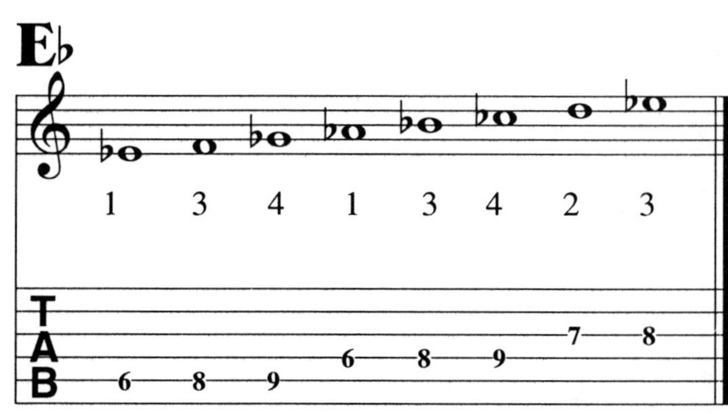

E

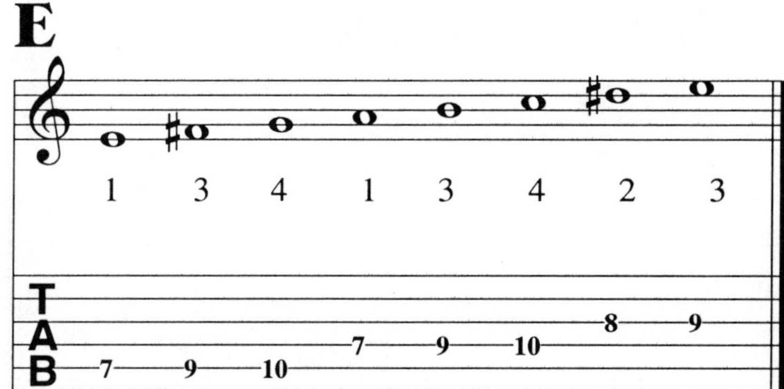

F

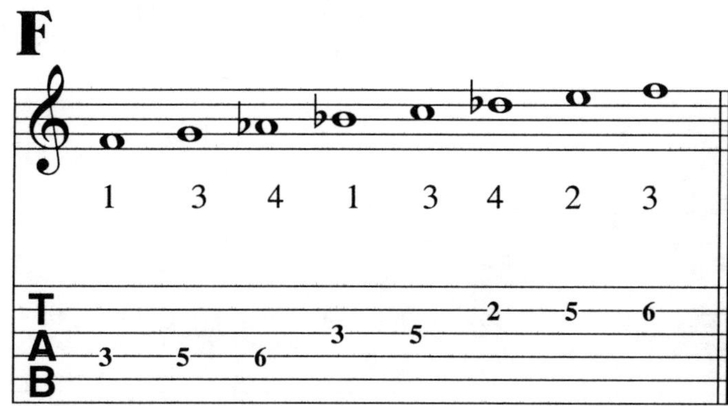

F♯

G

A♭

A

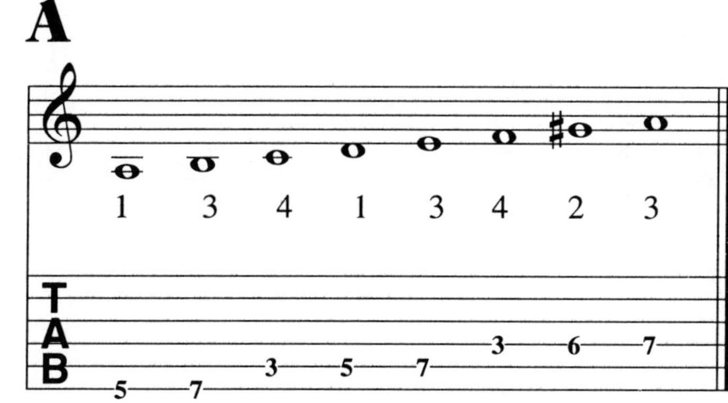

B♭

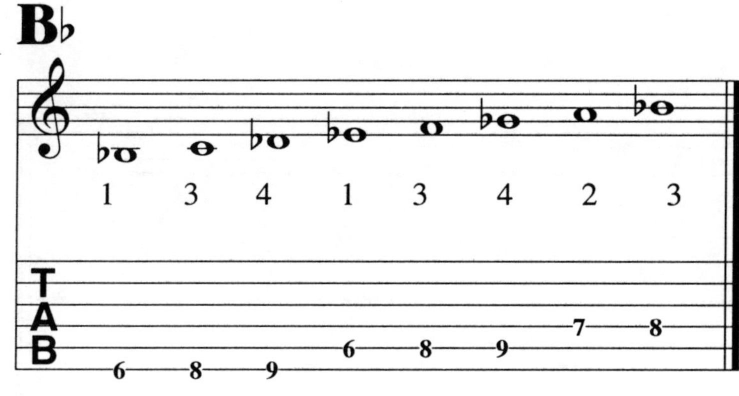

B

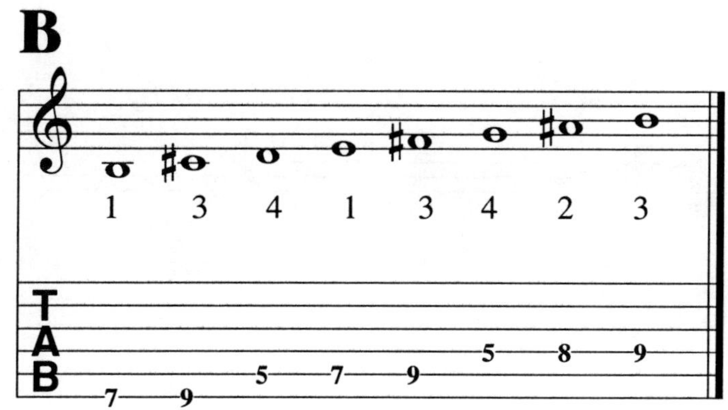

☆☆

RHYTHM STUDIES

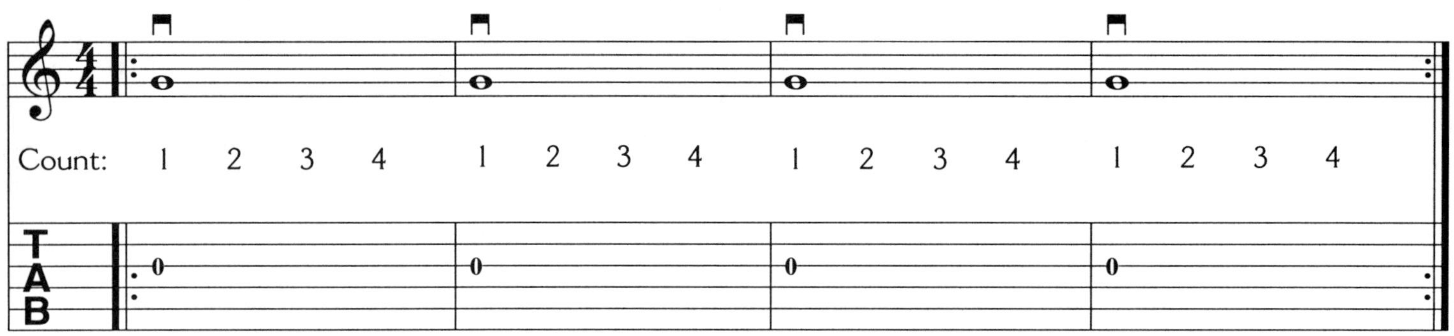

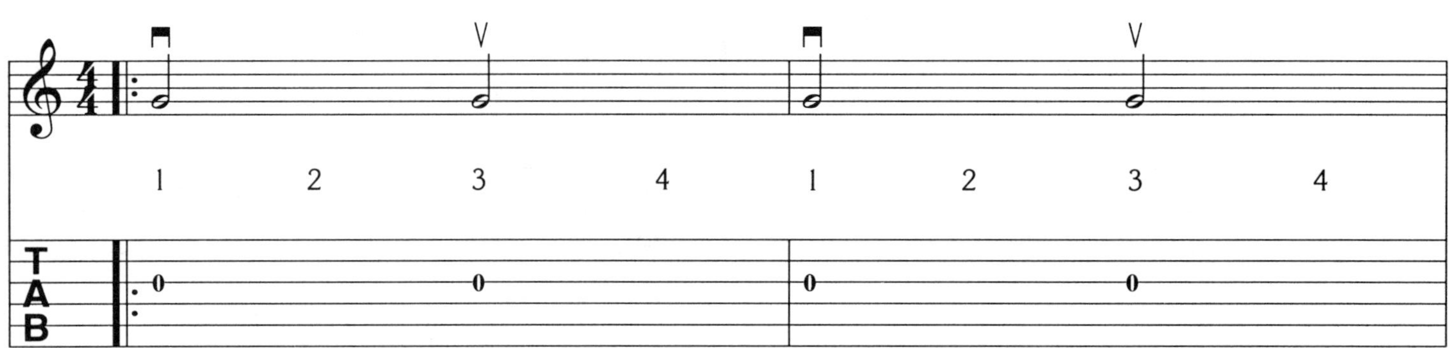

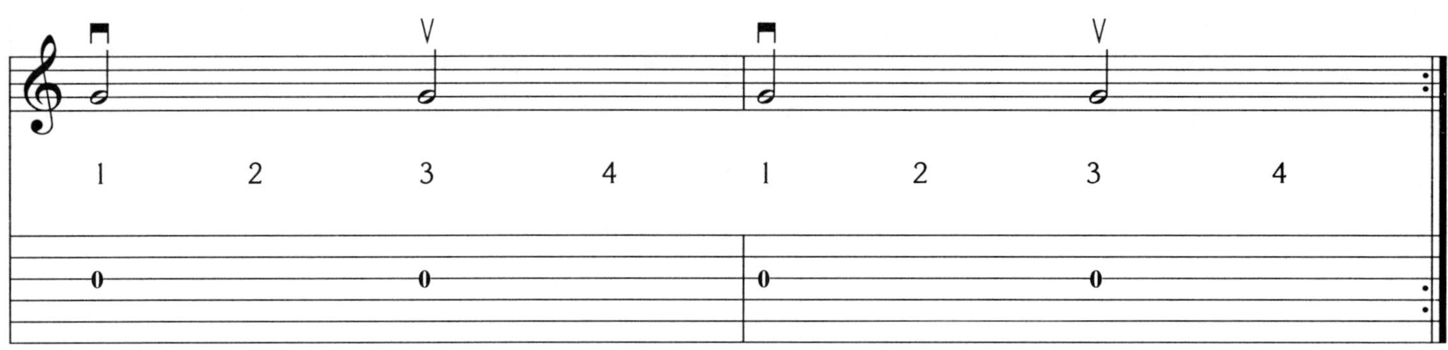

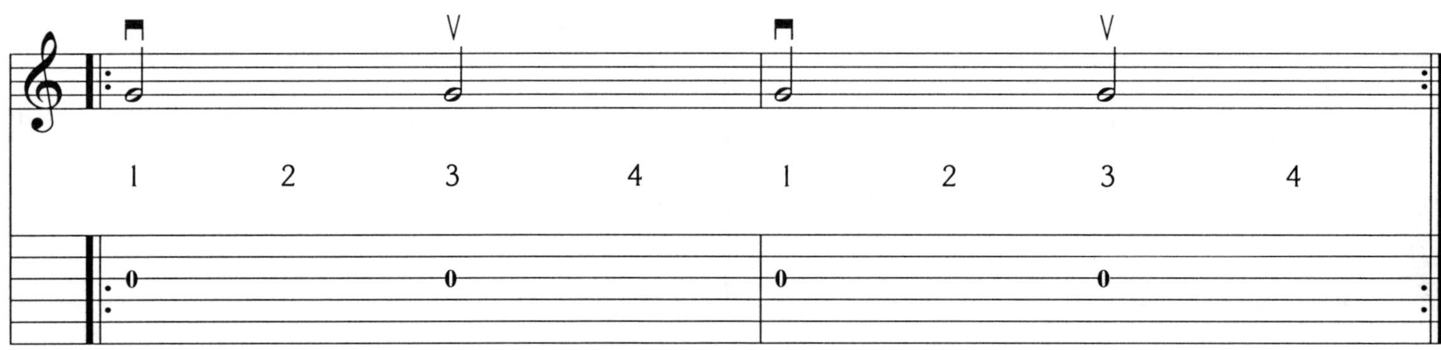

Count: 1 2 3 4 1 2 3 4
1 2 3 4 1 2 3 4
1 & 2 & 3 & 4 & 1 & 2 & 3 & 4 & 1 & 2 & 3 & 4 & 1 & 2 & 3 & 4 &
1 e & a 2 e & a 3 e & a 4 e & a 1 e & a 2 e & a 3 e & a 4 e & a
1 e & a 2 e & a 3 e & a 4 e & a 1 e & a 2 e & a 3 e & a 4 e & a

☆☆

EXERCISE 1

A steady eighth note up and downstroke pattern is common practice.

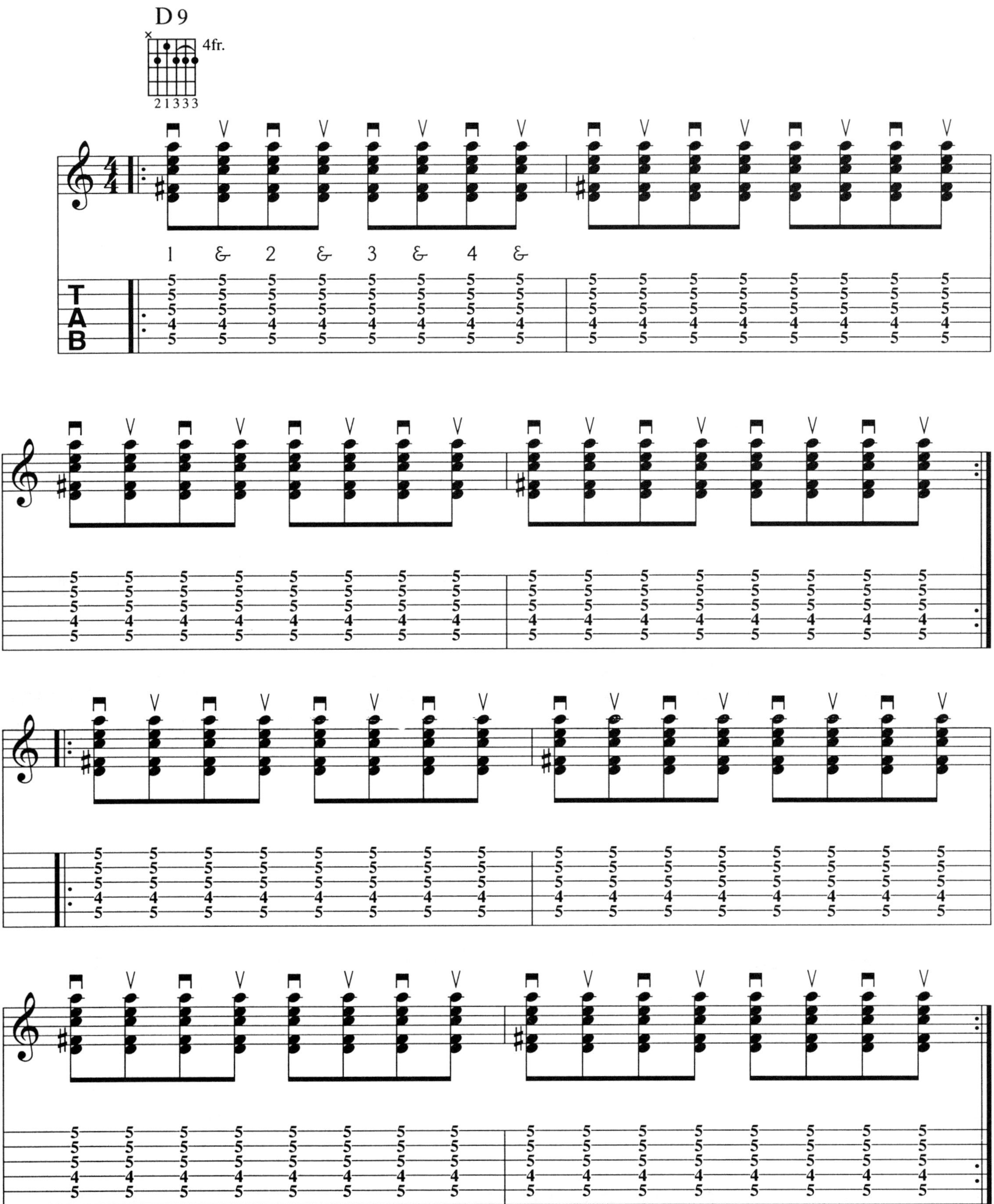

This symbol (–) is for the ***legato stroke*** (A stroke in which you keep pressure on the string with your left or fingerboard hand letting the strings fully sound on and in between strokes.).

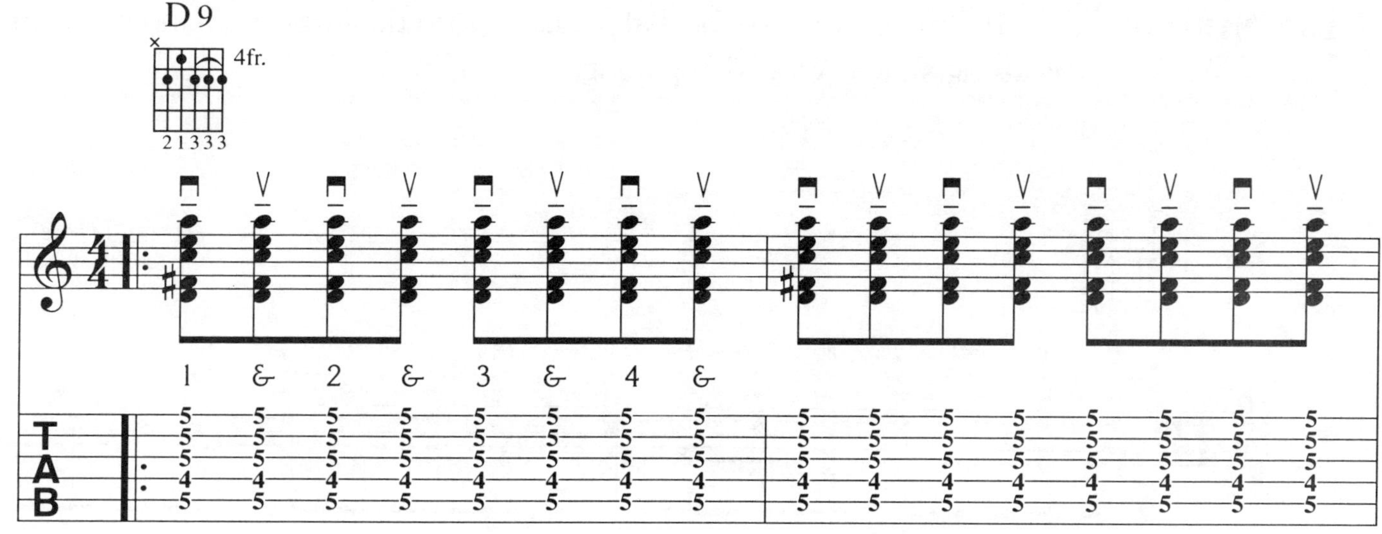

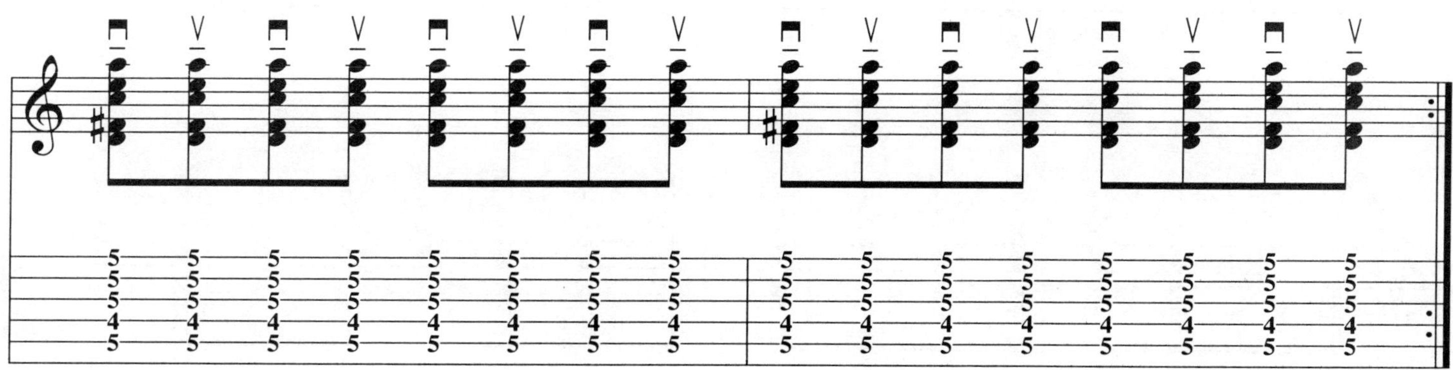

Exercise 2

Staccato Mark (·) = means to play each note short.

Dead Stroke = (♪) this means to apply partial pressure with the fingering hand while stroking the string(s), known as dampening.

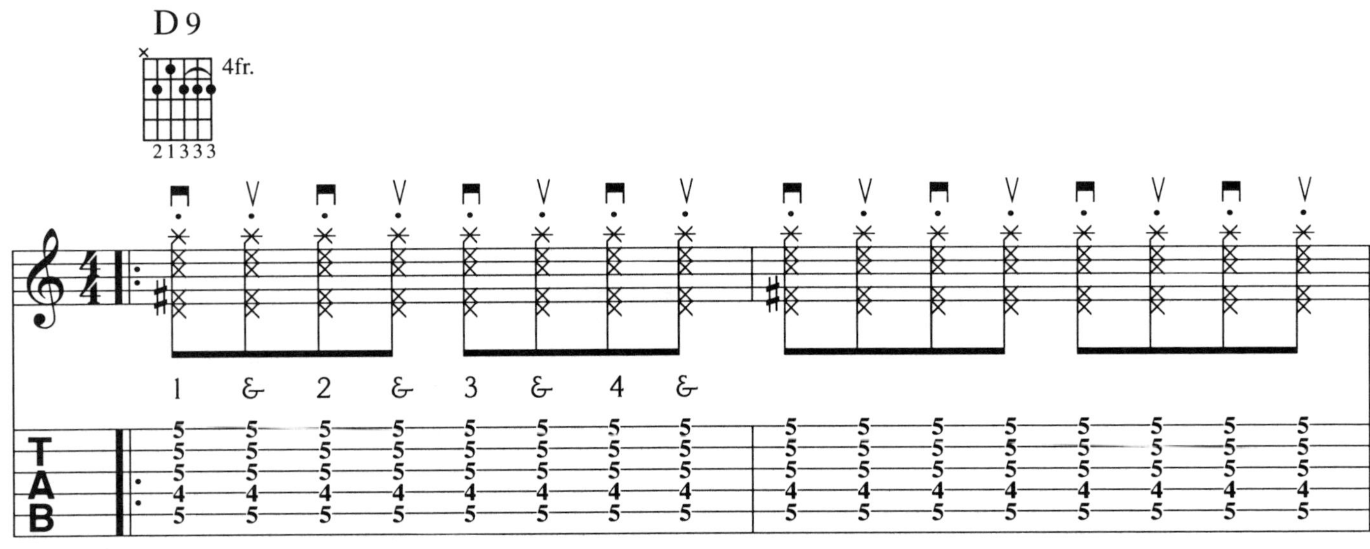

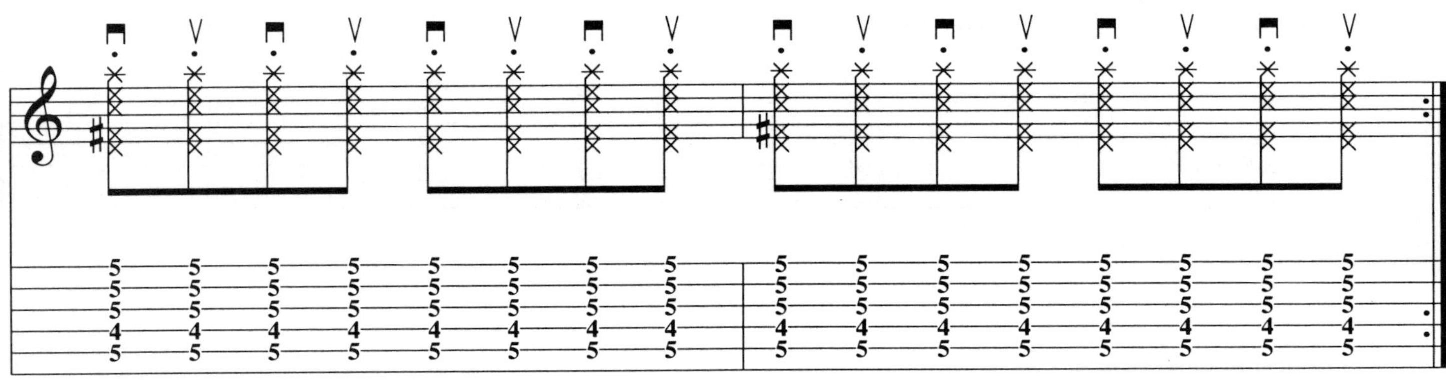

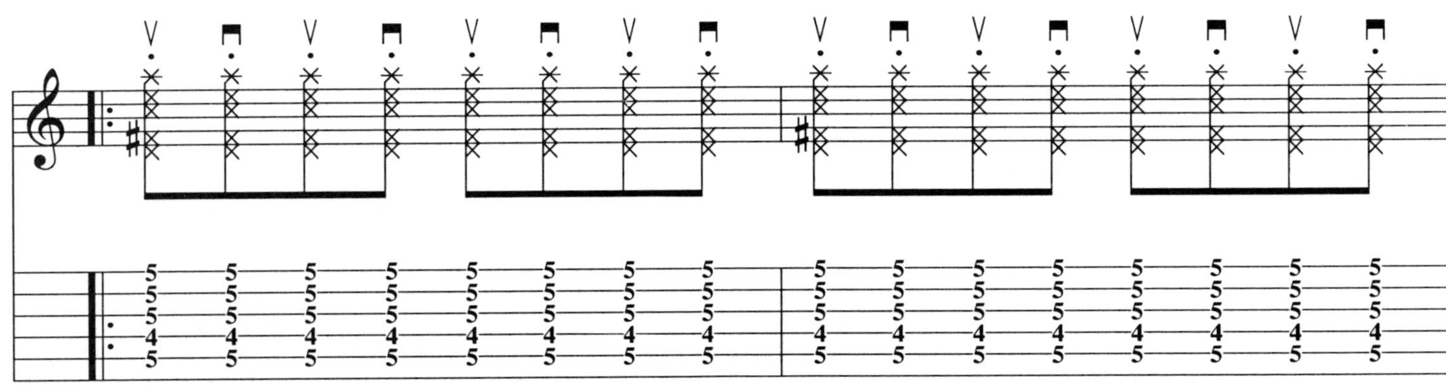

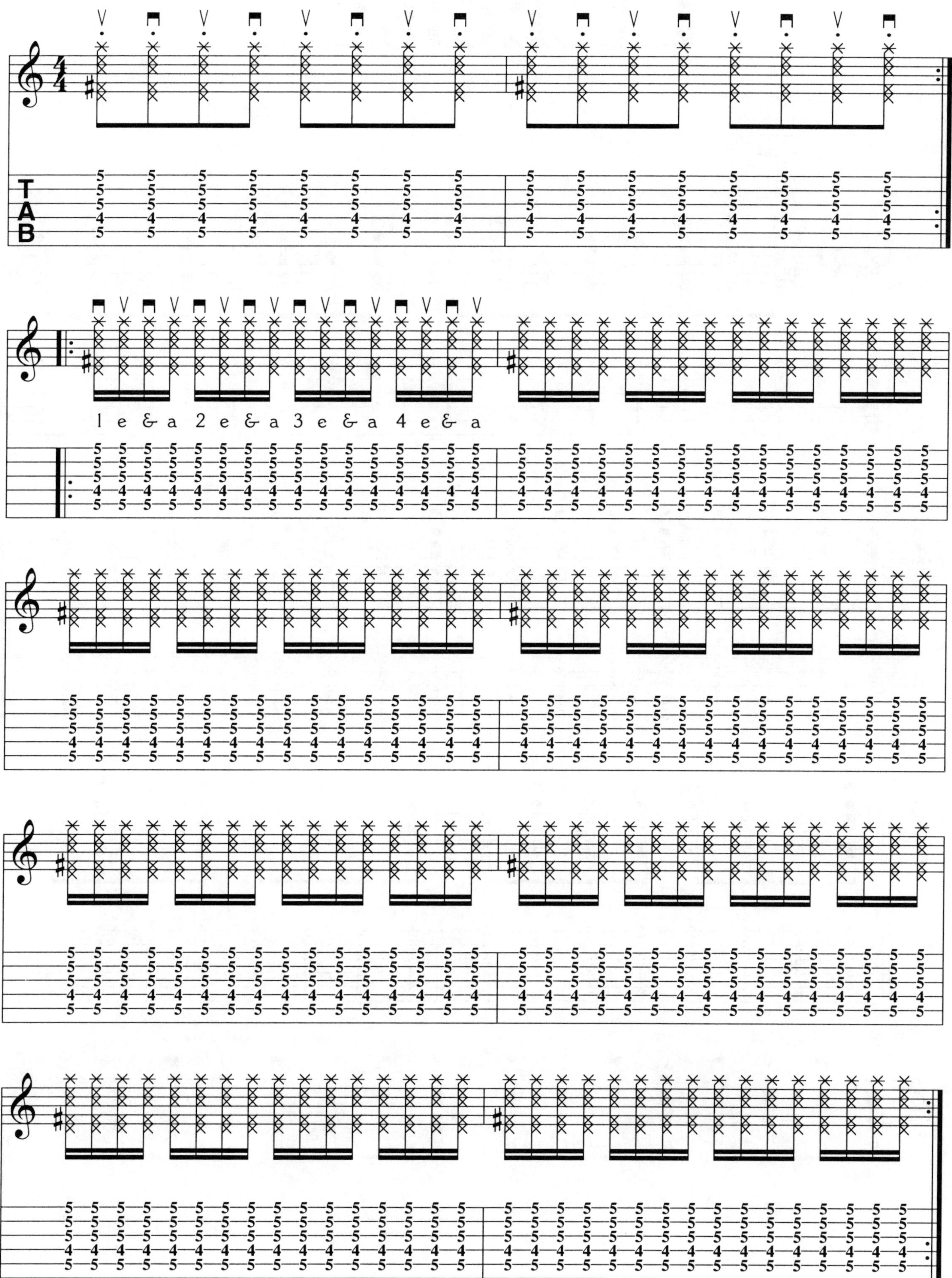
1 e & a 2 e & a 3 e & a 4 e & a

Exercise 3

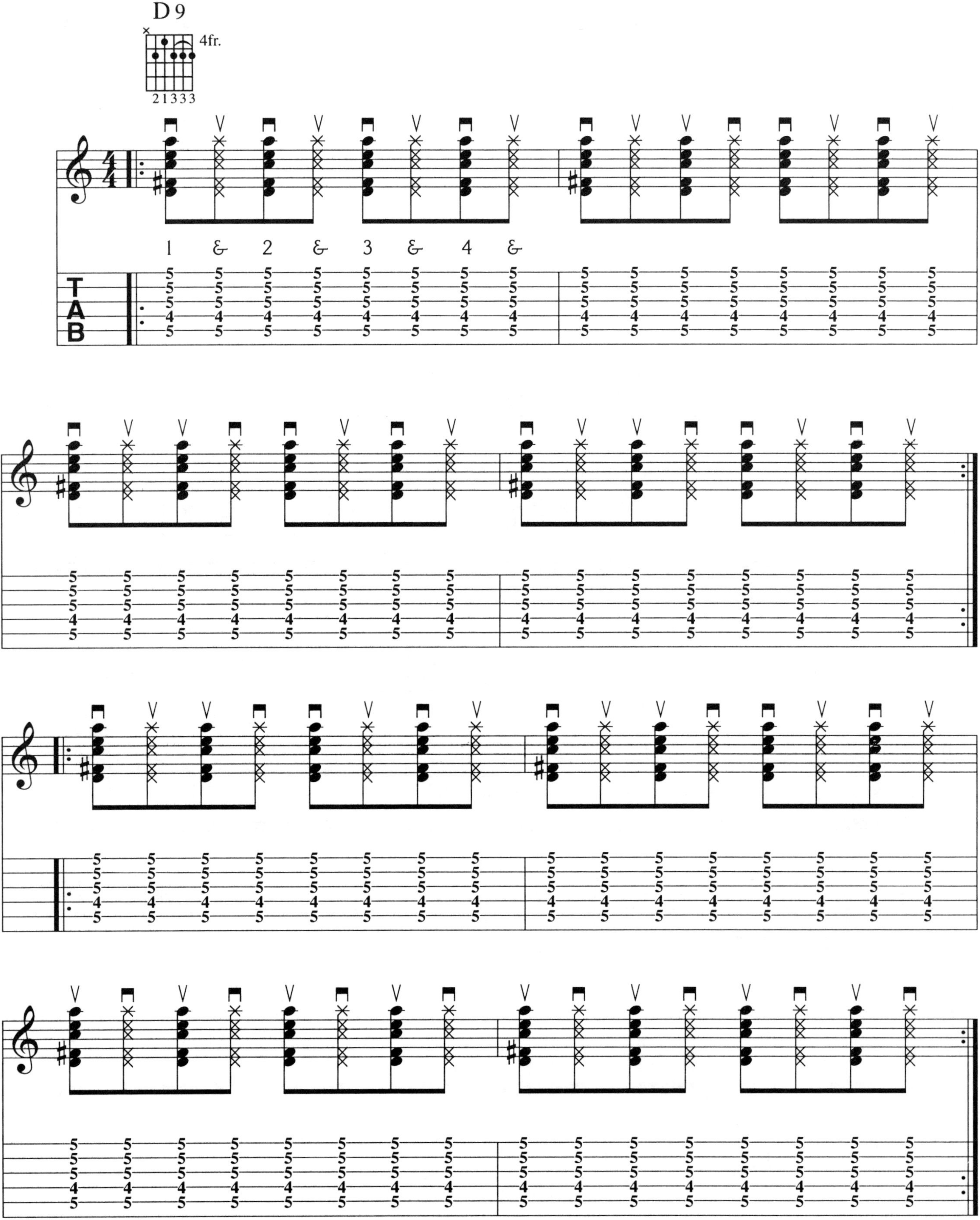

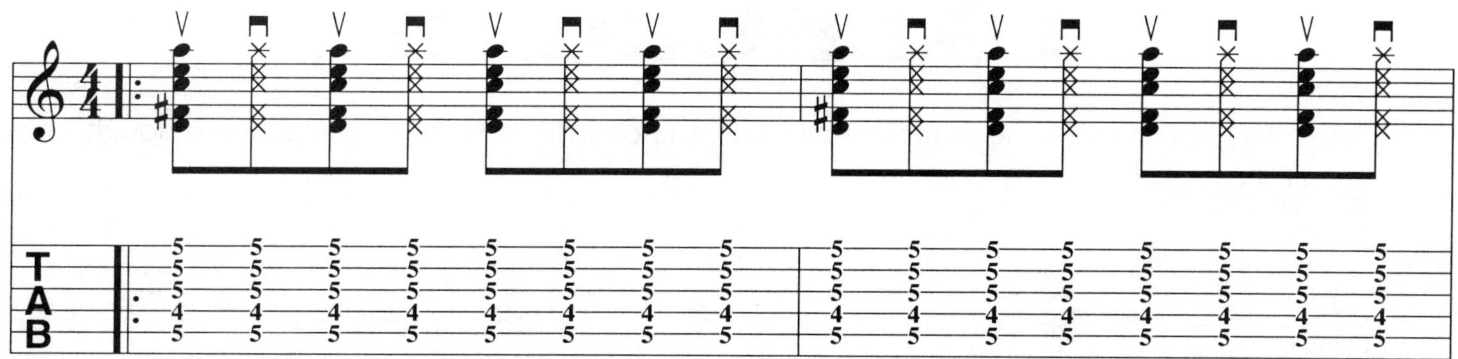

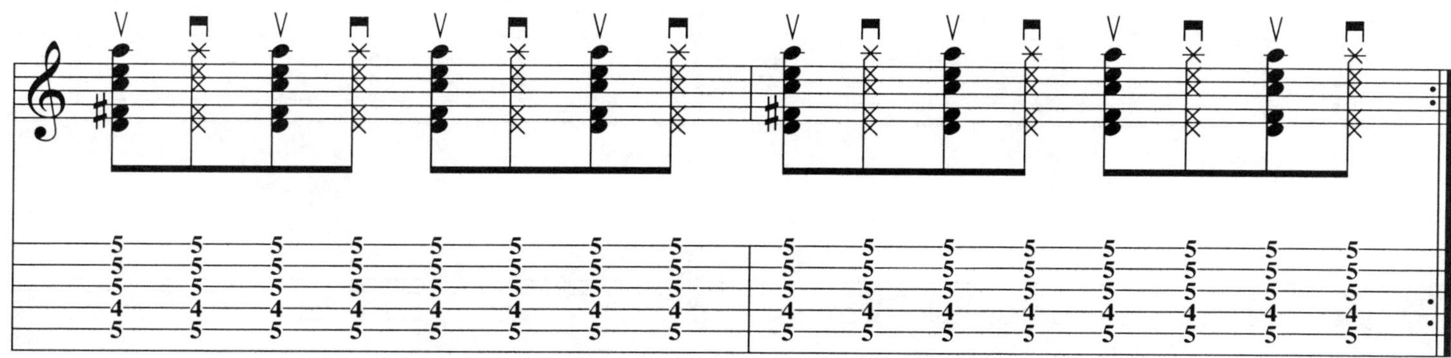

EXERCISE 4

Exercise 5

Note: To get the left-hand dampening effect, the chord has to be fingered even though only two notes fully sound.

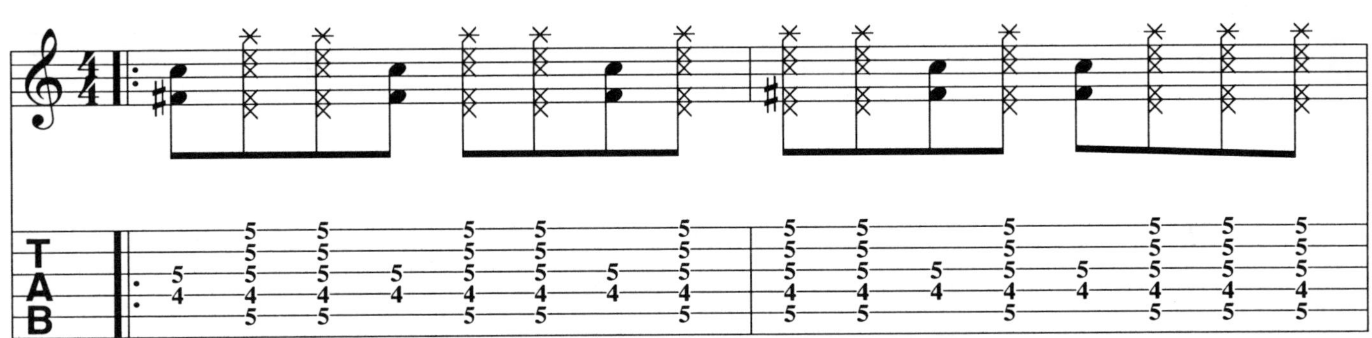

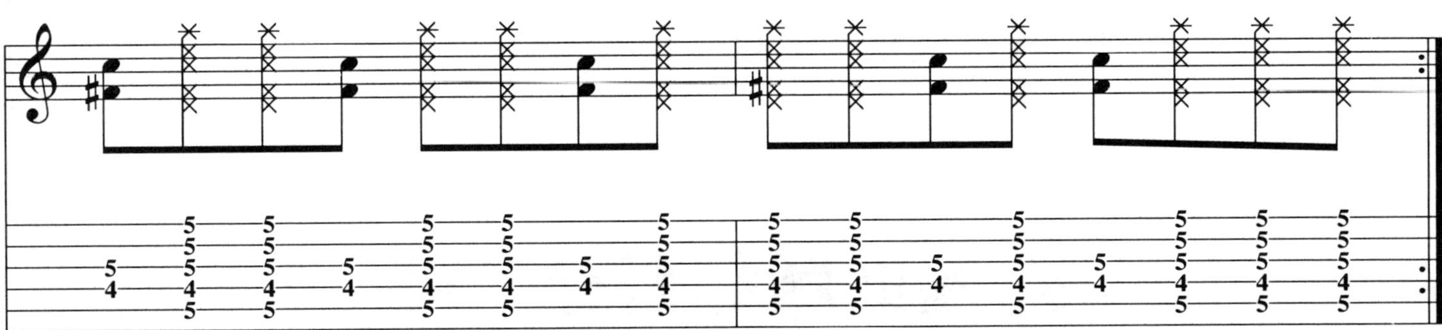

Exercise 6

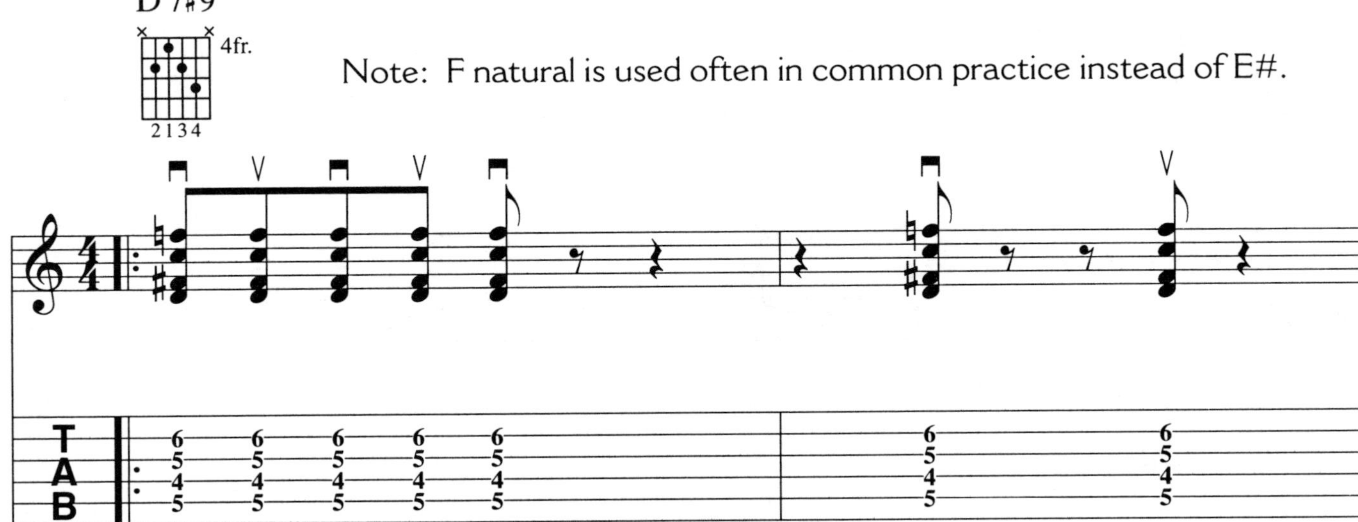

Note: F natural is used often in common practice instead of E#.

EXERCISE 7

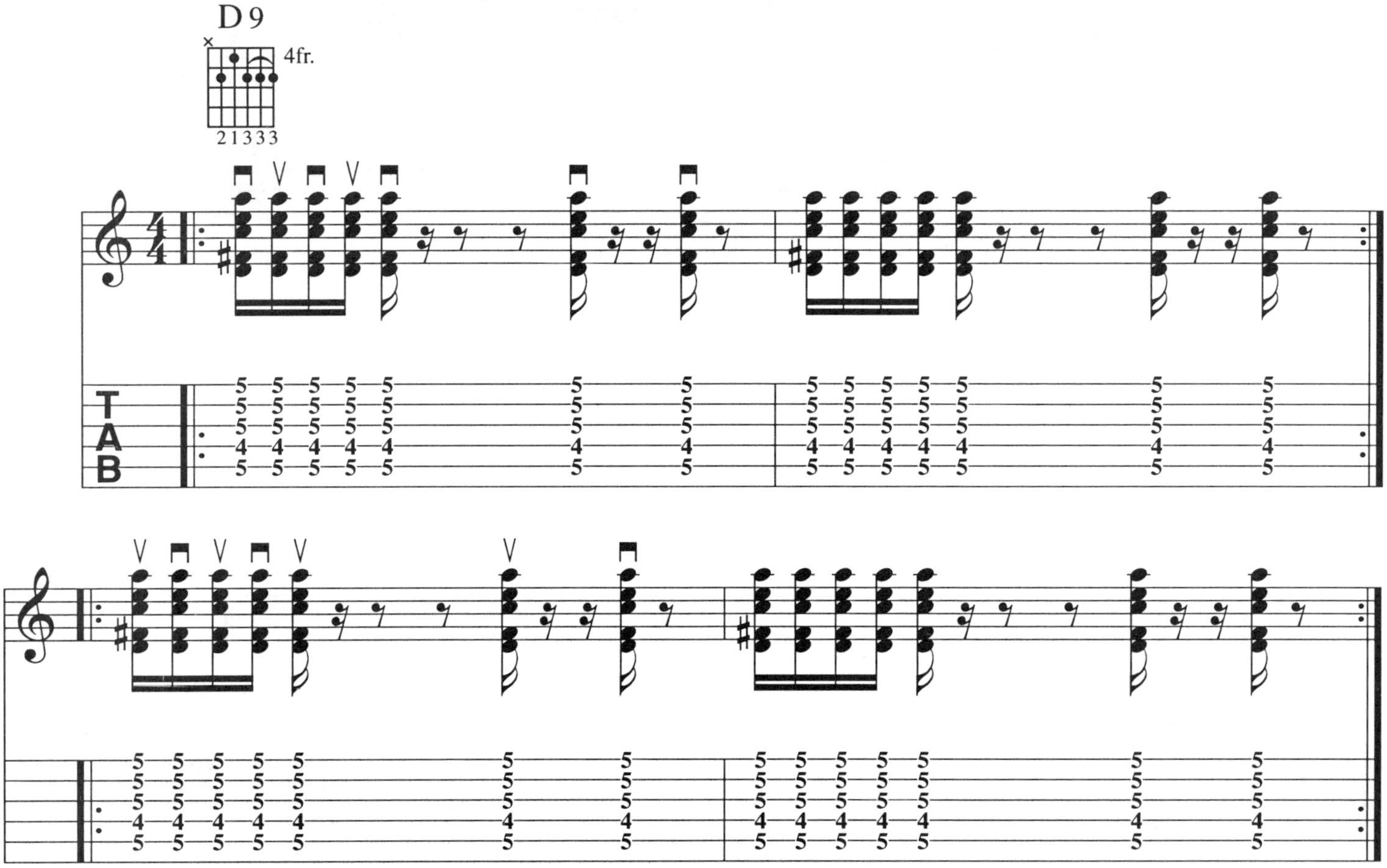

D9

4fr.

21333

EXERCISE 8

Note: The slide here consists of two notes. The first note is the only one attacked.

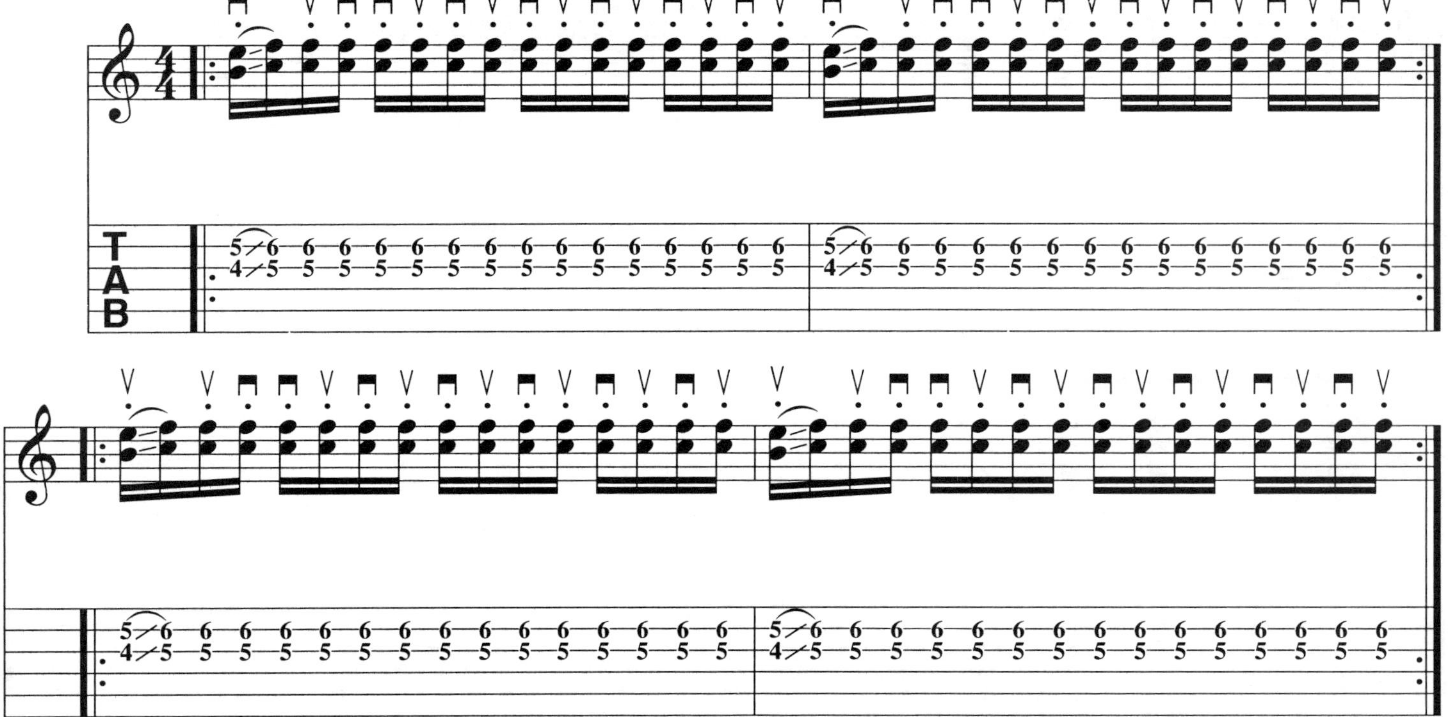

Exercise 9

Right or Pick-Hand Dampening (Palm-Muting)

The fleshy part of the palm as shown touches the strings(s) just enough to keep the string(s) from vibrating fully.

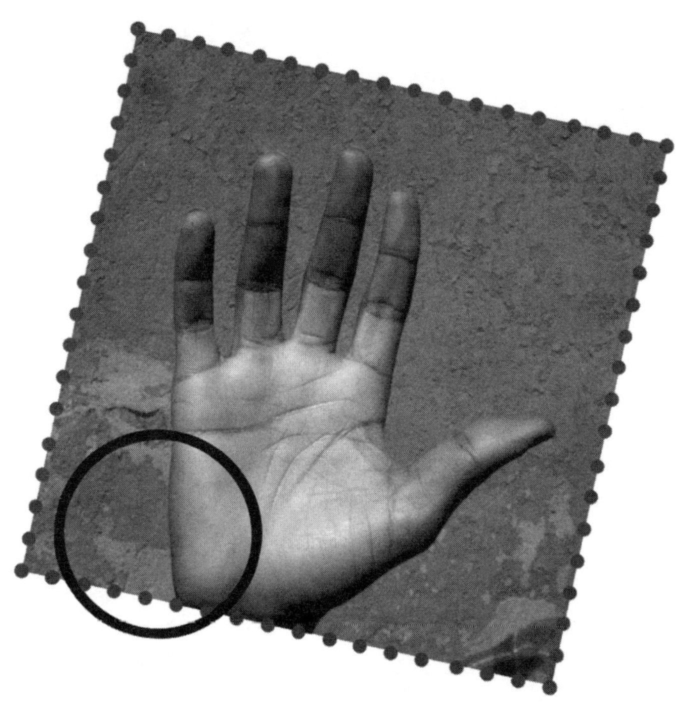

Exercise 10

Note: Pick-hand dampening (Palm Muting) can be applied to most examples and etudes.

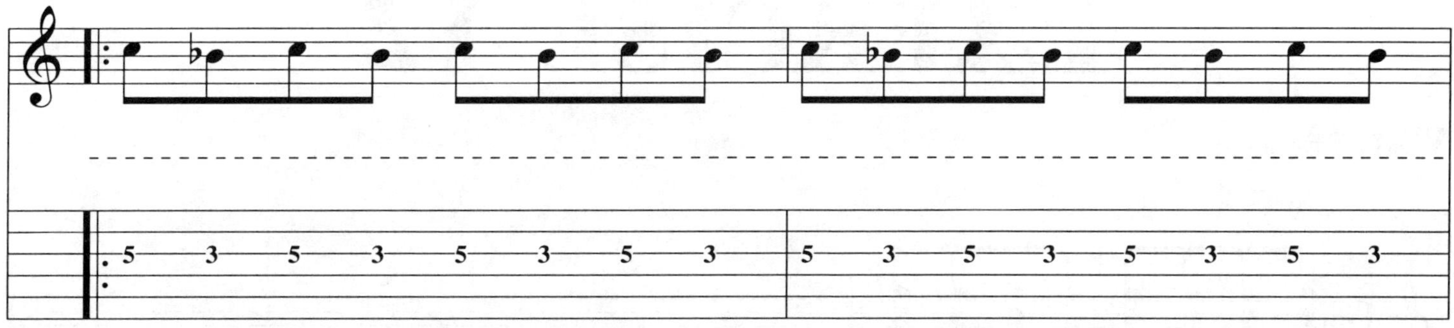

To master this technique, play all of the scales presented at the beginning of the book in this manner.

EXERCISE 11

These are some of the ways a written chord chart appears in common practice.

WRITTEN:

OR:

PLAYED:

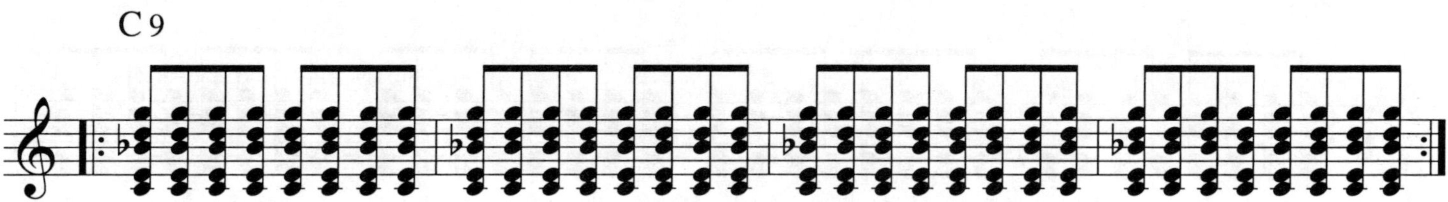

Exercise 12

Written:

(Repeat previous measure)

Played:

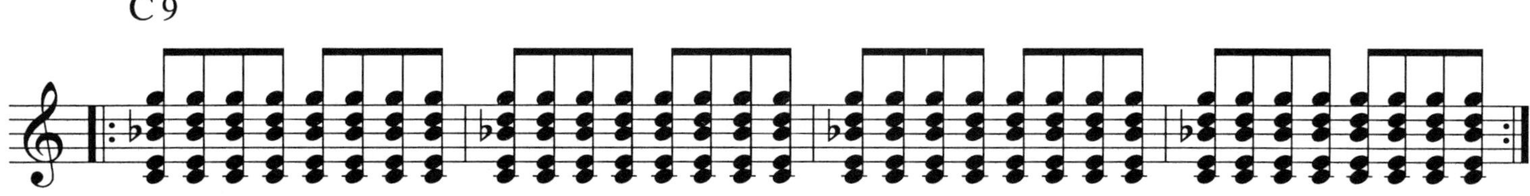

Written:

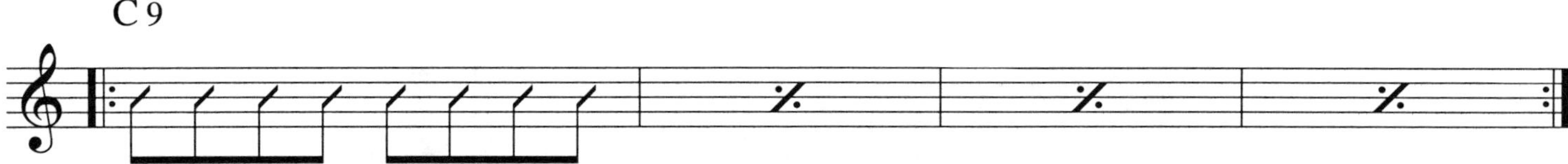

Played:

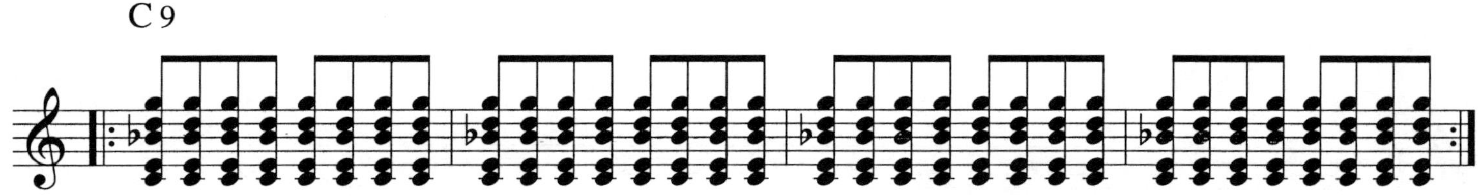

Written:

(Repeat previous two measures)

Played:

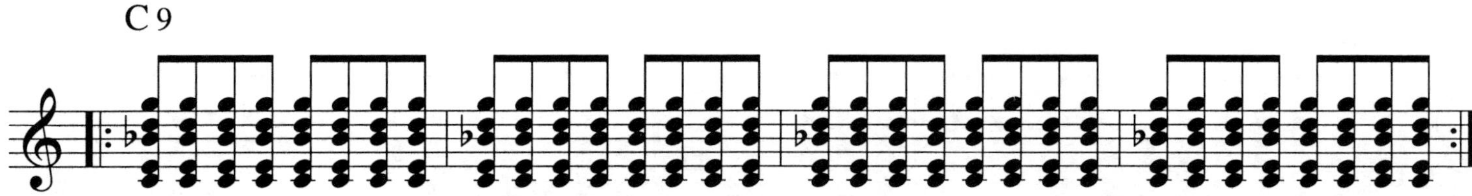

The Wah-Wah Pedal

The wah-wah pedal, although experiencing a current comeback, was commonly used in the late 60's and 70's. It is a device that electronically simulates the "plunger effects" that are common to jazz brass players when they cover and uncover the bell of the horn while playing making the ooh-wah sound. The wah pedal was popularized by Jimi Hendrix's solo albums and the numerous Motown recordings of Wah Wah Watson.

Note: Don't pat or keep time with the pedal foot, the goal is control. You should stand comfortably with most of your weight shifted to the off pedal foot.

The Symbols Under the Notes

O = Open (maximum up position)

X = Closed (maximum down position)

H = Half open (half up position)

EXERCISE 13

Note: Rhythms can be played on the pedal while the fingered note(s) is held.

x o x o o x o x
1 2 3 4 1 2 3 4 1 2 3 4 1 2 3 4
T
A
B
8 8 8 8
5 5 5 5

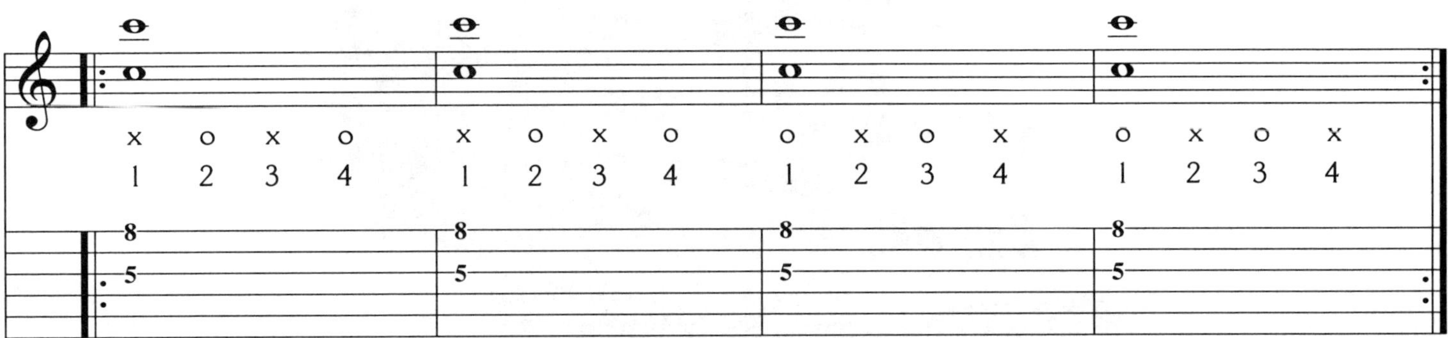

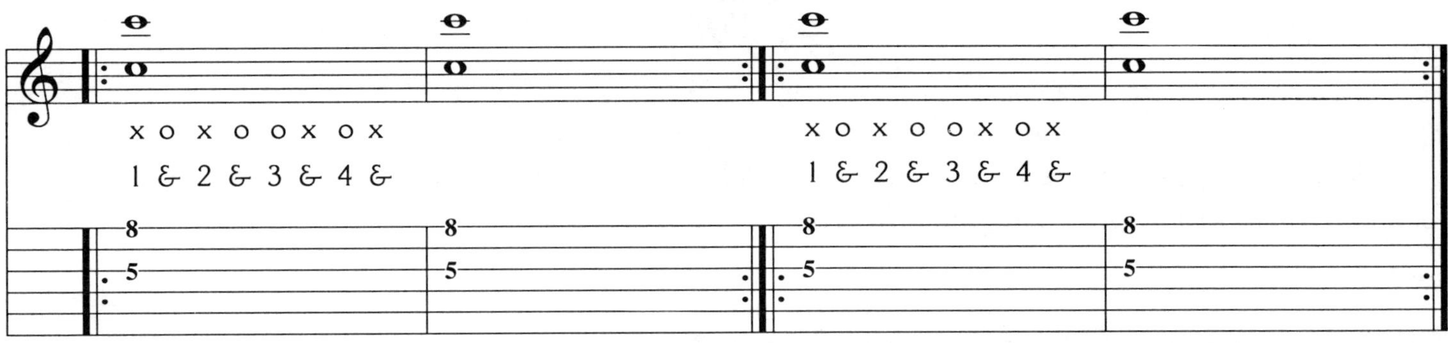

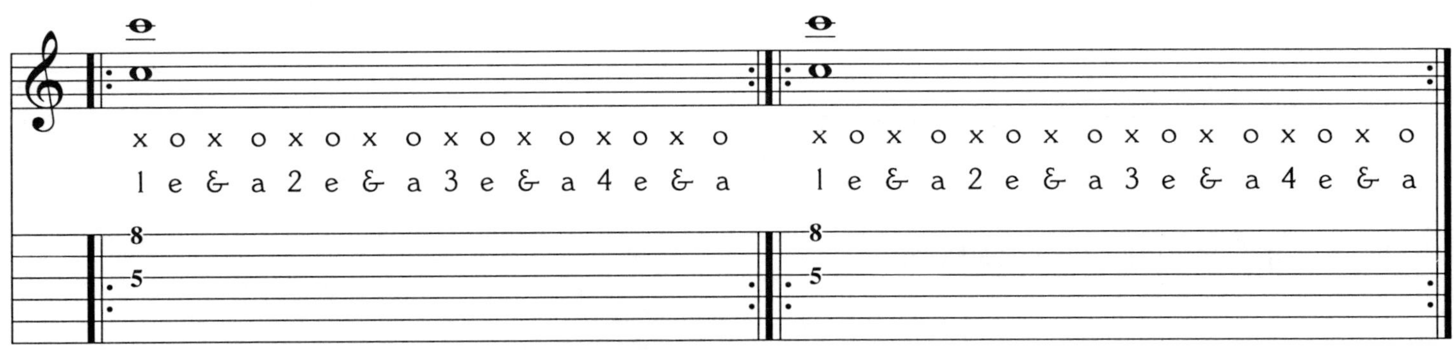

Exercise 14

Note: Use legato stroke with all examples.

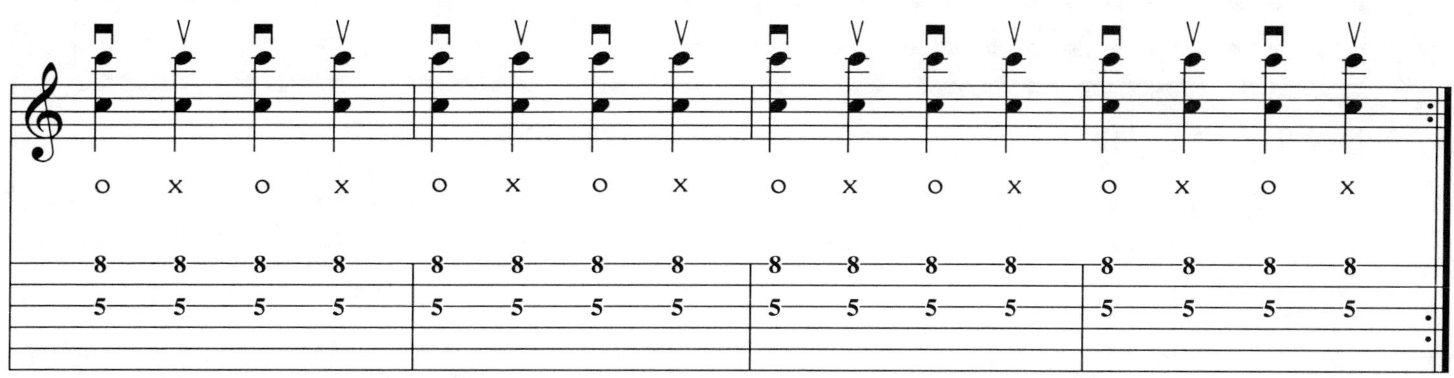

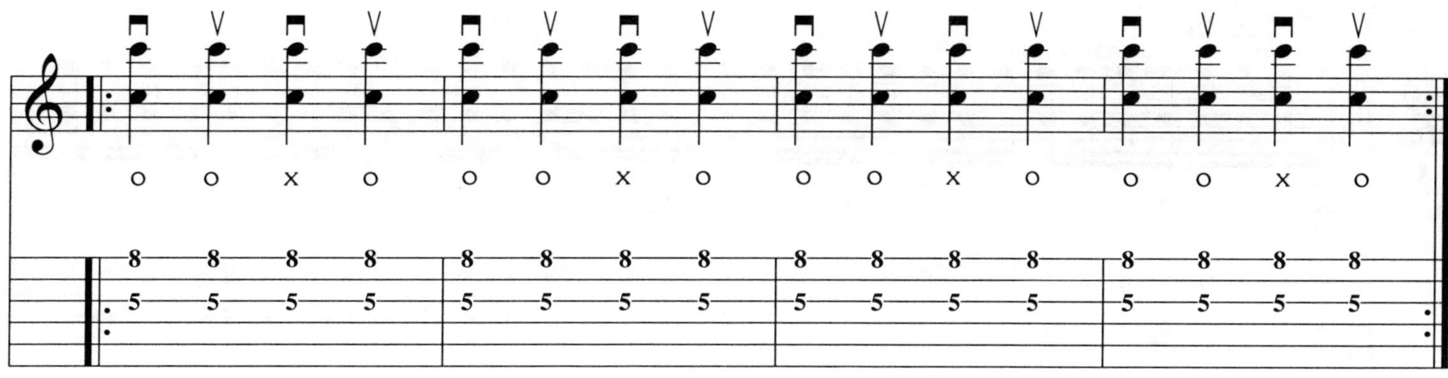

Exercise 15

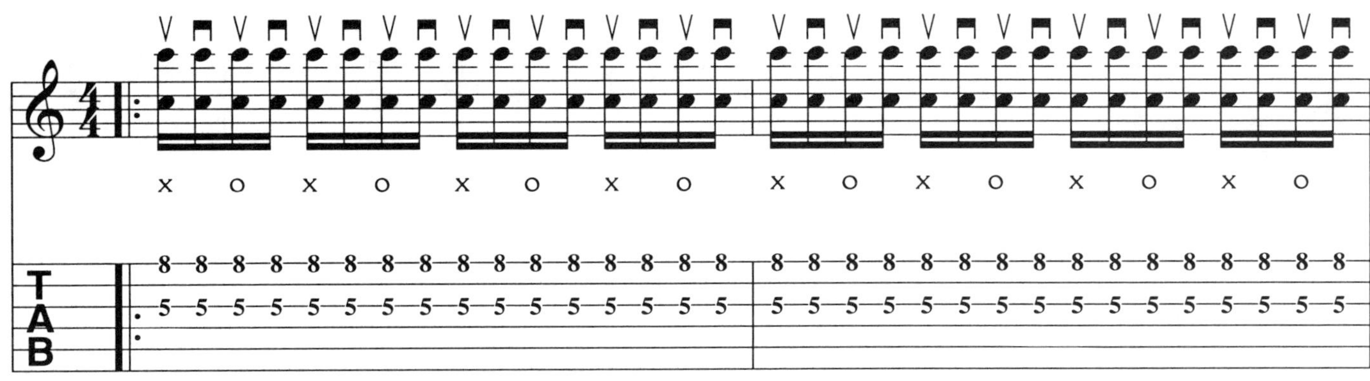

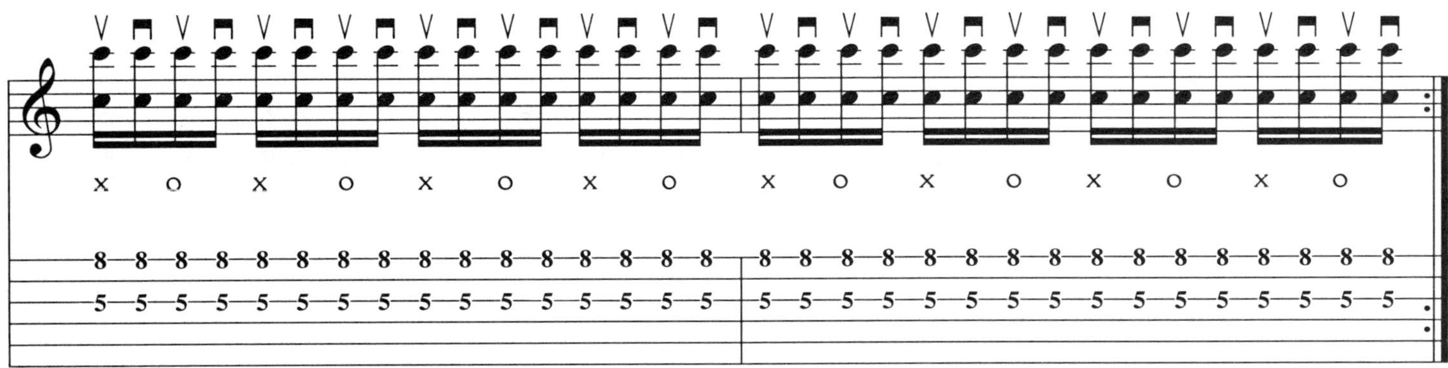

Exercise 16

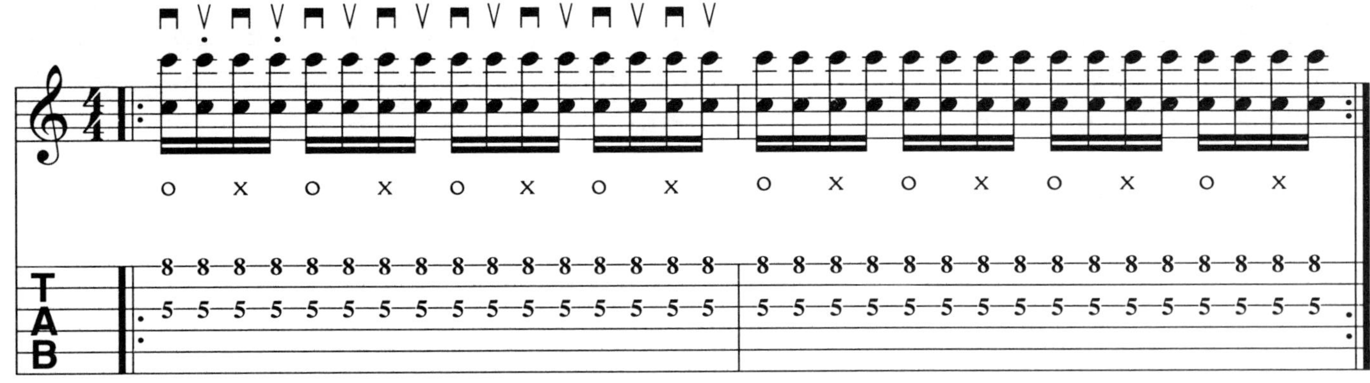

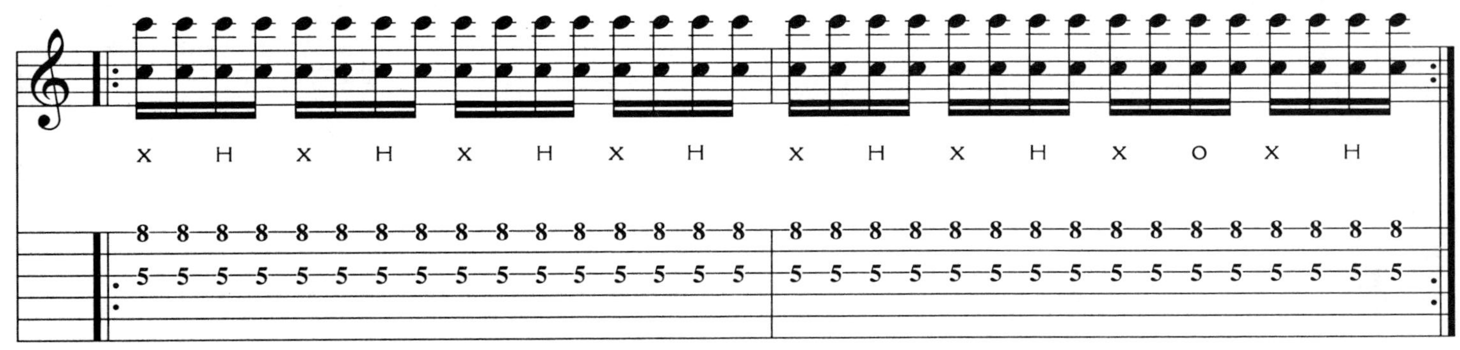

EXERCISE 17

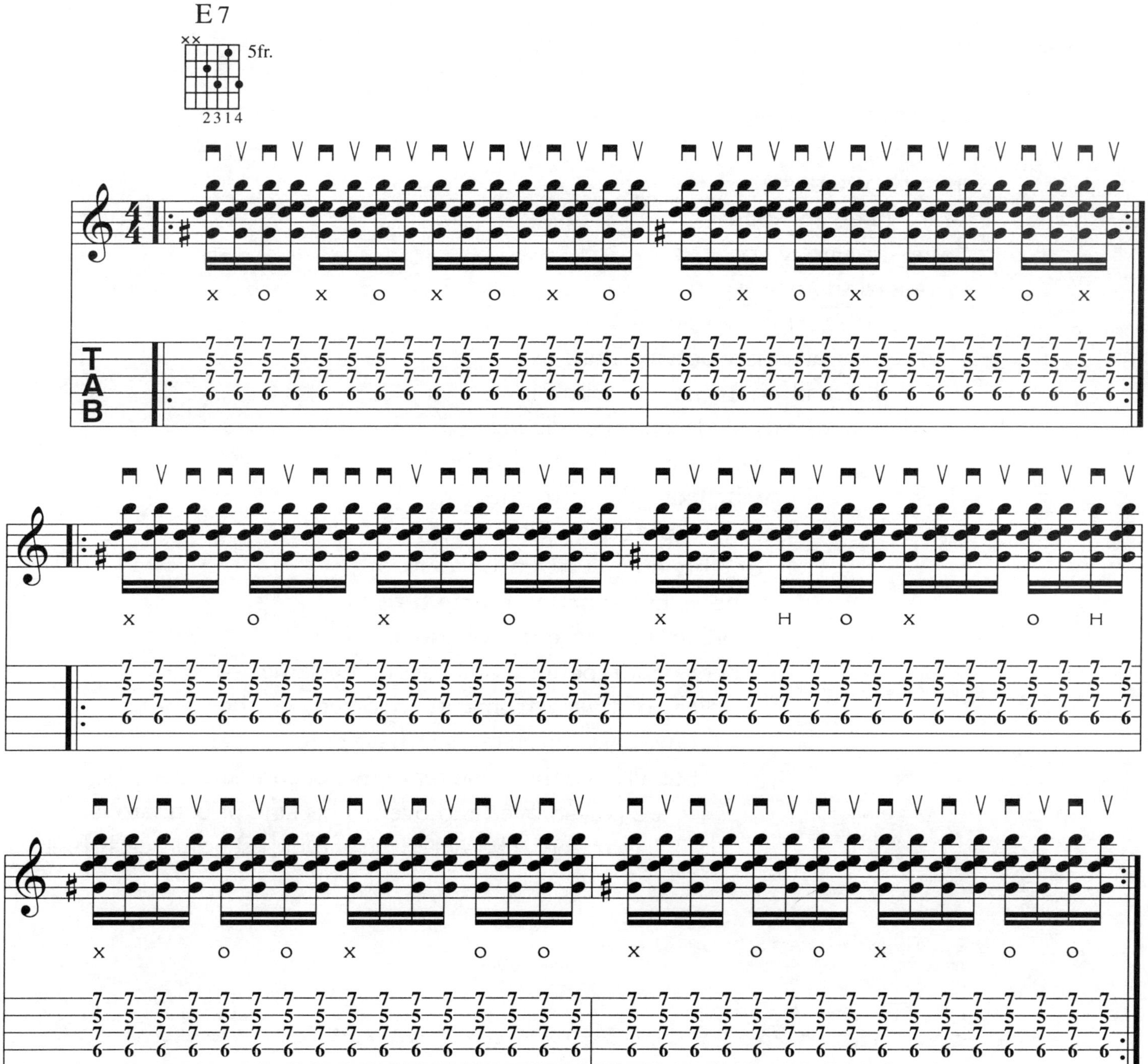

E7

5fr.

2314

FUNK OF THE 60'S, 70'S AND 80'S

James Brown created most of the common practices in the early funk era (late 60's). Often two guitars were used to keep the integrity of the record and/or live performance. The two guitars would alternate between single line and chord parts. Funk in each of these decades has distinctive characteristics. Our goal in the following examples is to show the common practices "in the style of"this era. Within borders of the richly syncopated texture of funk music is the use of ostinato (the persistent repetition of a part in the same voice) of the instruments involved, ie. the drums, bass and guitar each have different parts but all have the same repetitive occurances that are played over and over. This kind of ostinato is extremely characteristic of funk; especially early funk.

☆☆

In the Style Of

Playing this "Hambone" rhythm over a 12 bar blues will help you get into the idea of repetitious rhythm patterns.

1

Please Note: some examples do not have a recorded counterpart and some recordings do not have a written counterpart try to look and/or listen to those examples and play the best feel that is in context with the suggested style.

One type of syncopation shown in the following example is the ***hemiola*** which literally means 3 against 2. The following examples are in the style of James Brown.

This example is in the style of Kool and the Gang.

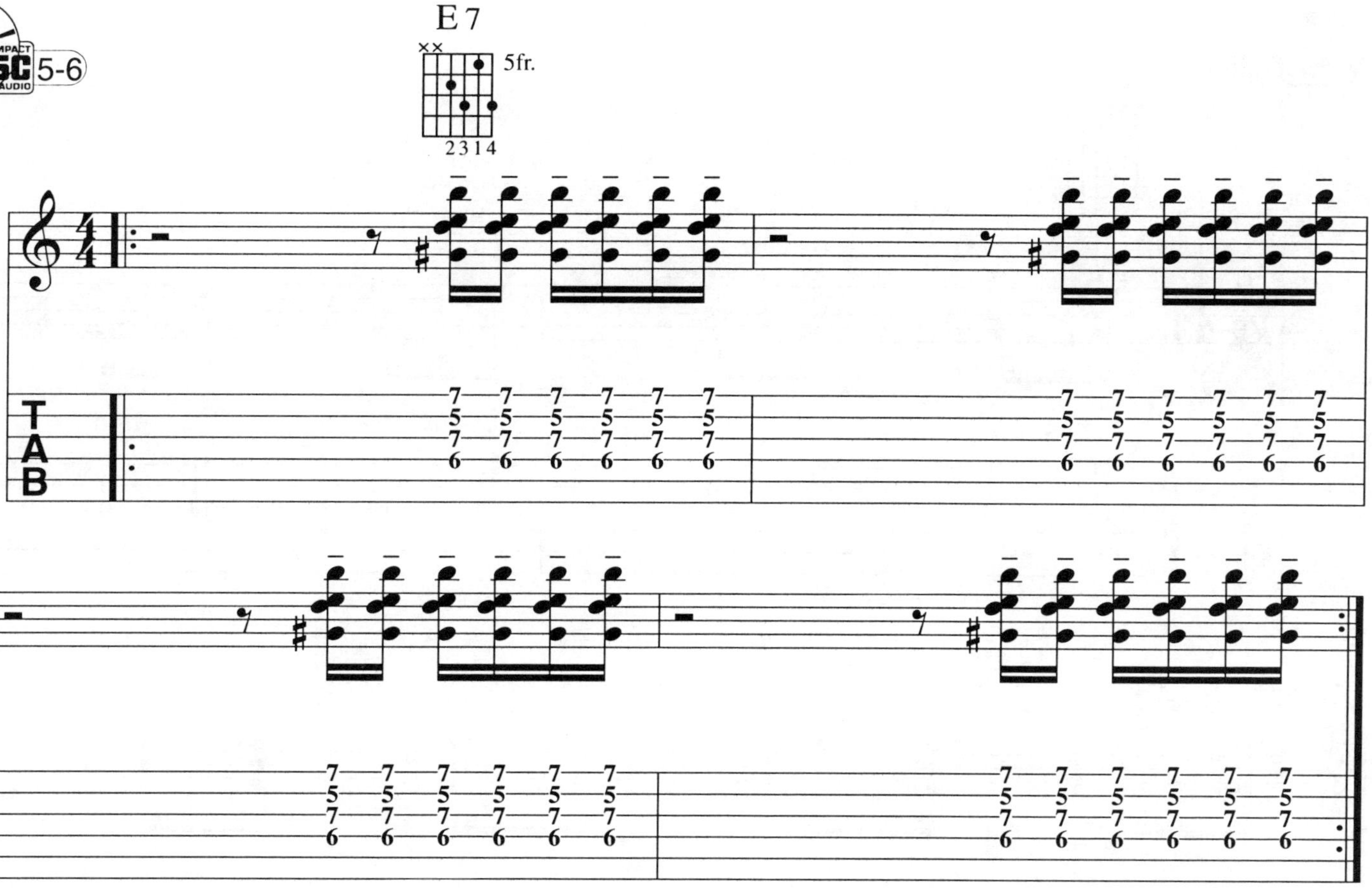

CD 5-6

E7

5fr.

2 3 1 4

This example is in the style of the Commodores.

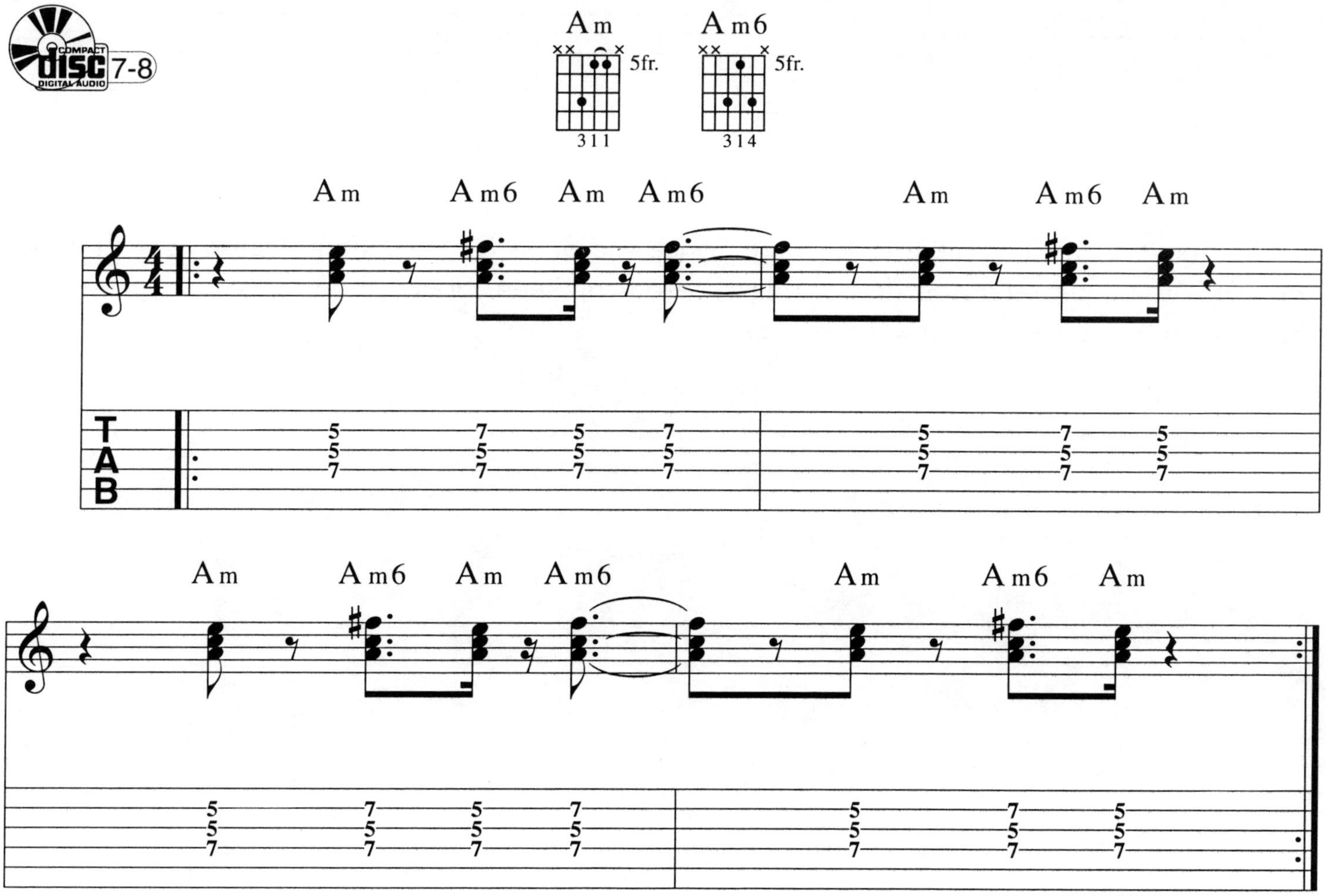

CD 7-8

Am 5fr. 3 1 1

Am6 5fr. 3 1 4

Am Am6 Am Am6 Am Am6 Am

Am Am6 Am Am6 Am Am6 Am

This example is in the style of the Zapp Band.

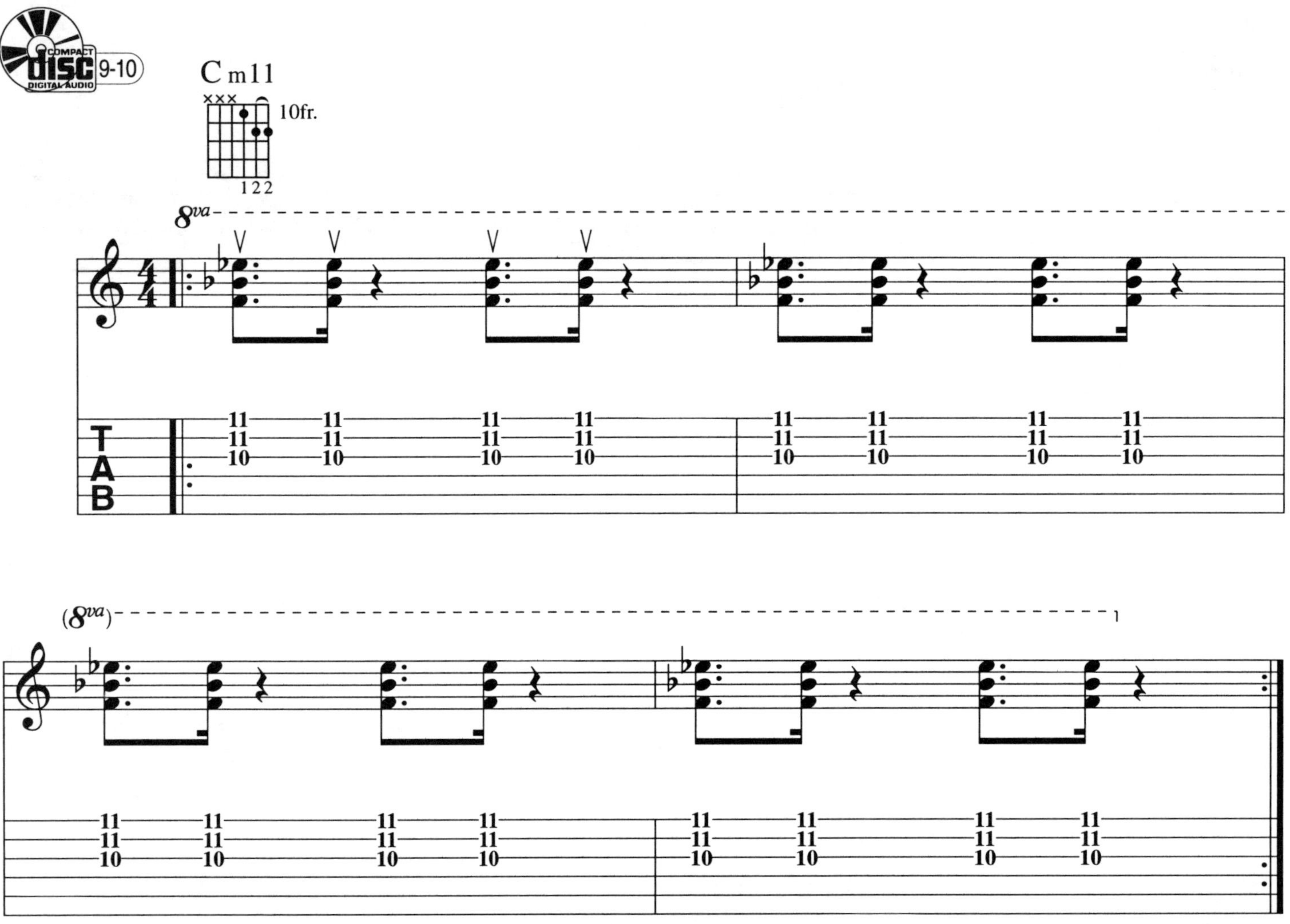

This next example is in the style of the Prince and Brass Construction. Please note that this example is to be played ***legato*** (left or fingerboard hand keeps pressure on the strings letting the notes sound fully on and in between strokes).

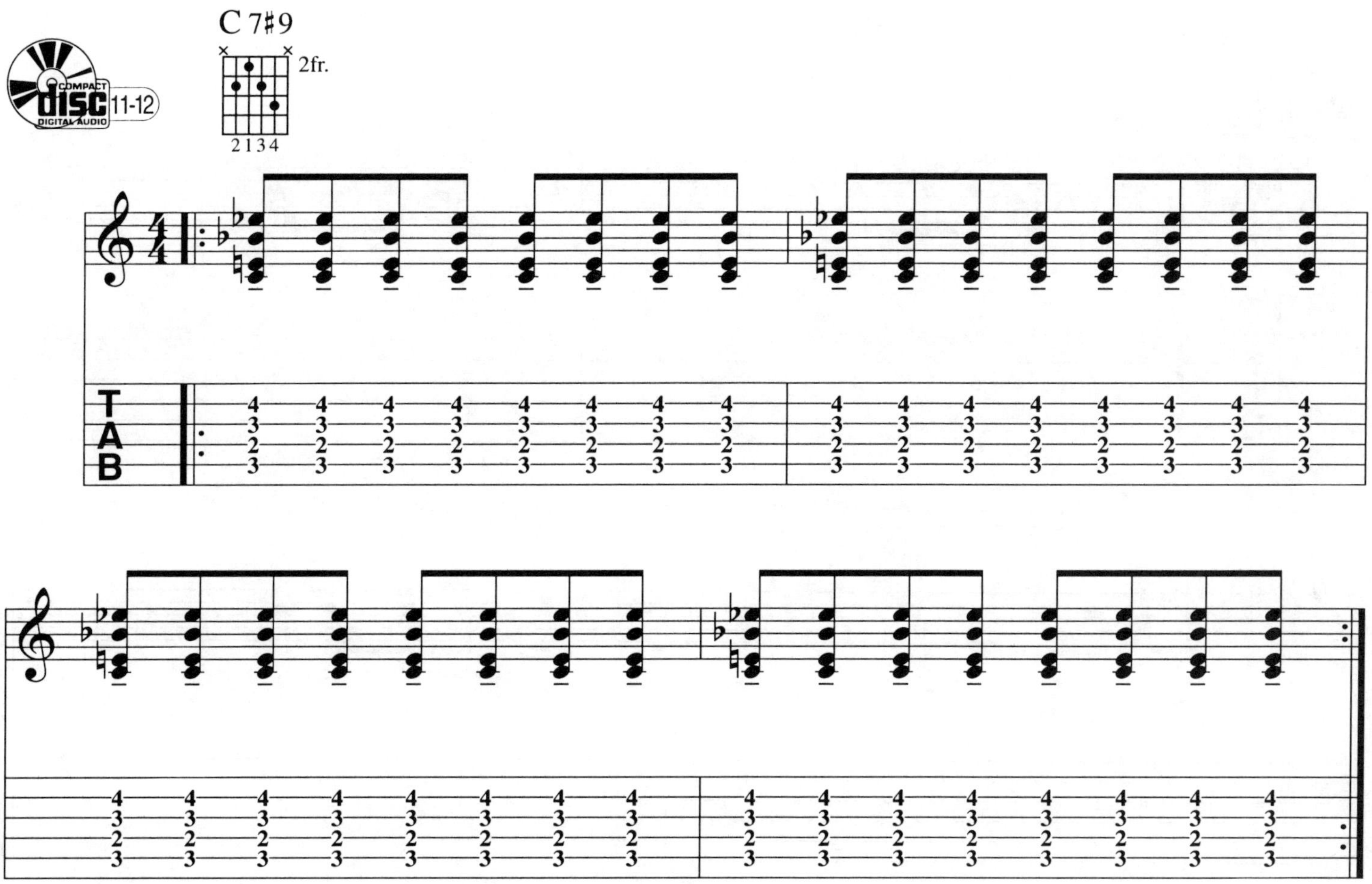

C 7#9

2fr.

2134

This example is in the style of Earth, Wind and Fire.

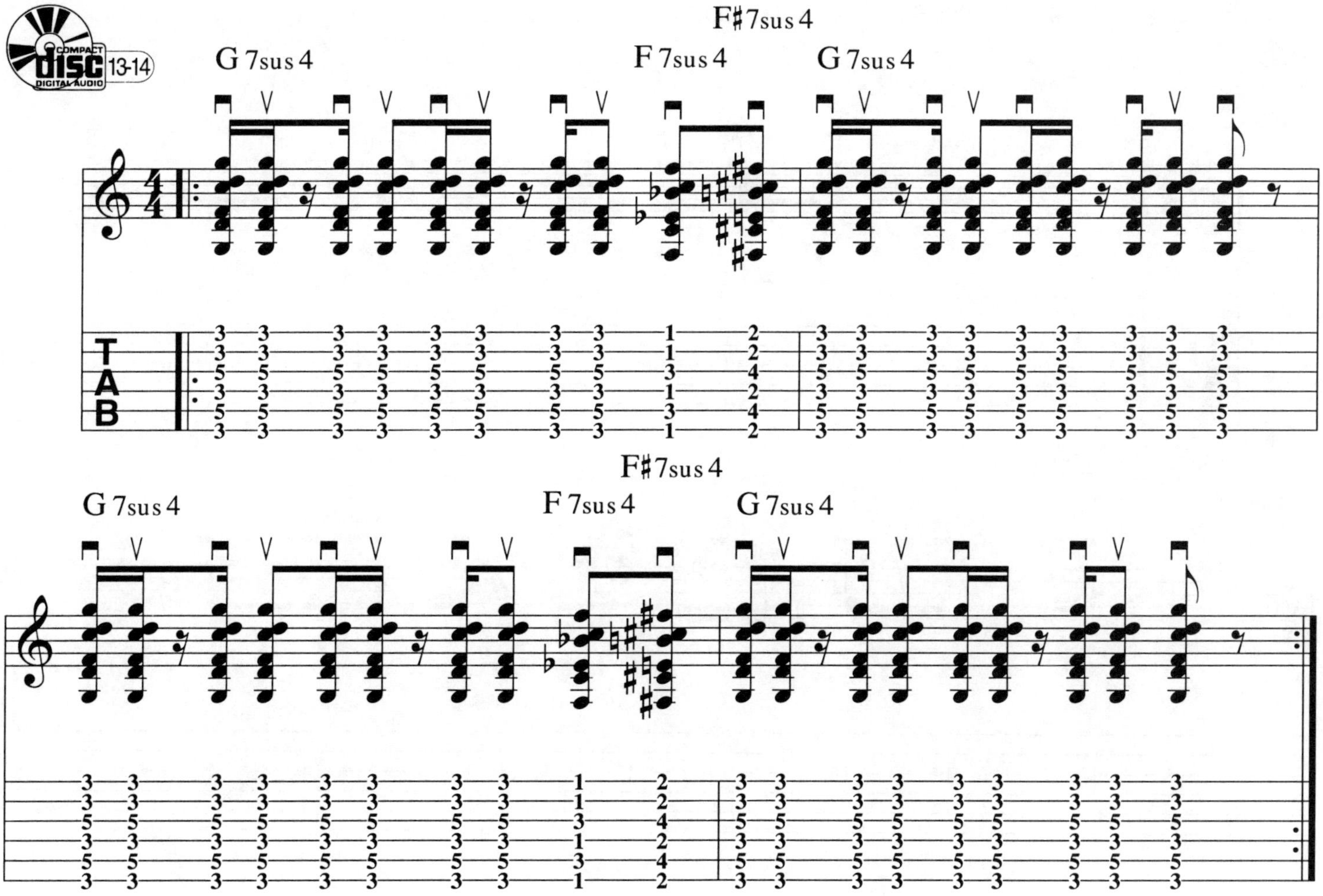

G 7sus 4 F#7sus 4 F 7sus 4 G 7sus 4

G 7sus 4 F#7sus 4 F 7sus 4 G 7sus 4

This example is in the style of the Average White Band.

This example is in the style of Rick James.

This example is in the style of Sly and the Family Stone.

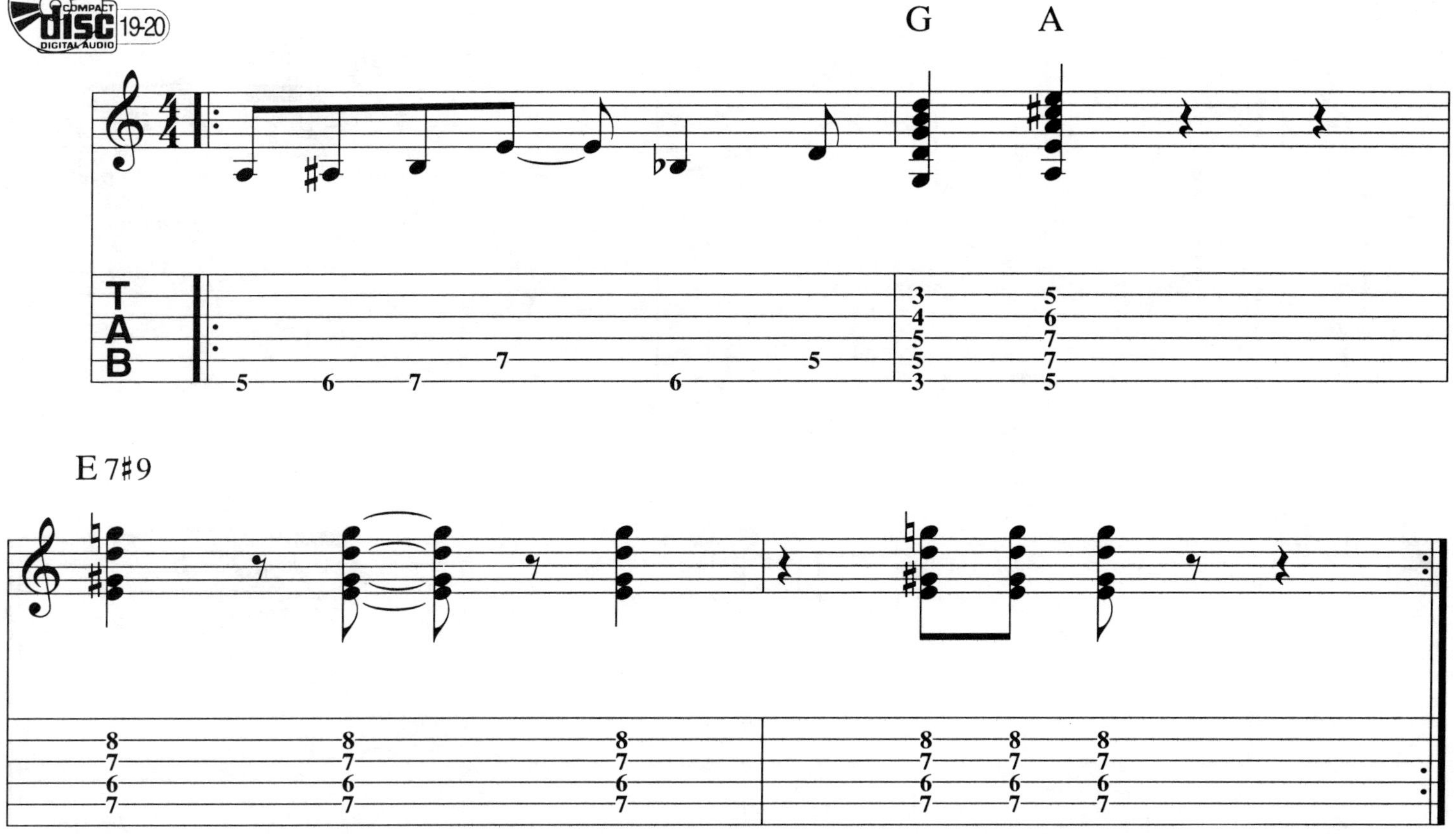

COMPACT disc DIGITAL AUDIO 19-20

G A

E 7♯9

This example is in the style of the Temptations.

COMPACT disc DIGITAL AUDIO 21

This example is in the style of the Gap Band.

This example is in the style of Cameo.

This example is in the style of War.

This example is in the style of LTD.

This example is in the style of Wild Cherry.

This example is in the style of B.T. Express.

This example is in the style of Tower of Power.

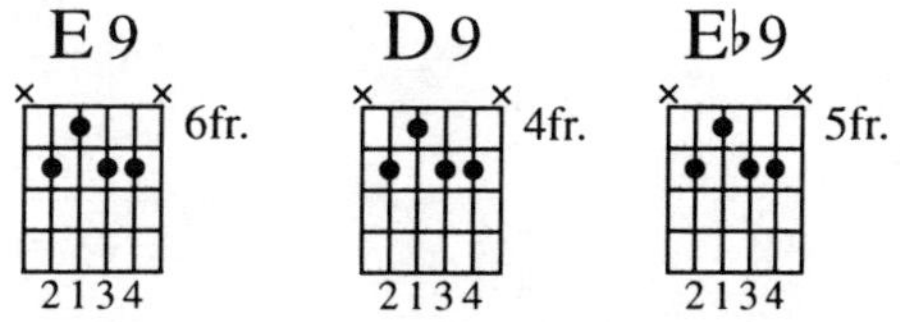

E9 (6fr., 2134) D9 (4fr., 2134) E♭9 (5fr., 2134)

E9 D9 E♭9 E9 D9 E♭9 E9

T
A
B

E9 D9 E♭9 E9 D9 E♭9 E9

This example is in the style of Rufus.

COMPACT DISC DIGITAL AUDIO 24

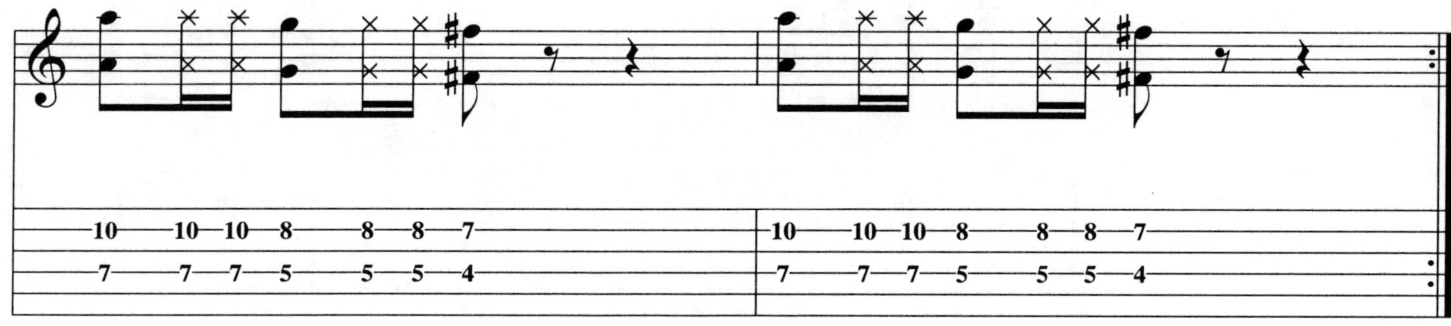

This example is in the style of Bootsy Collins.

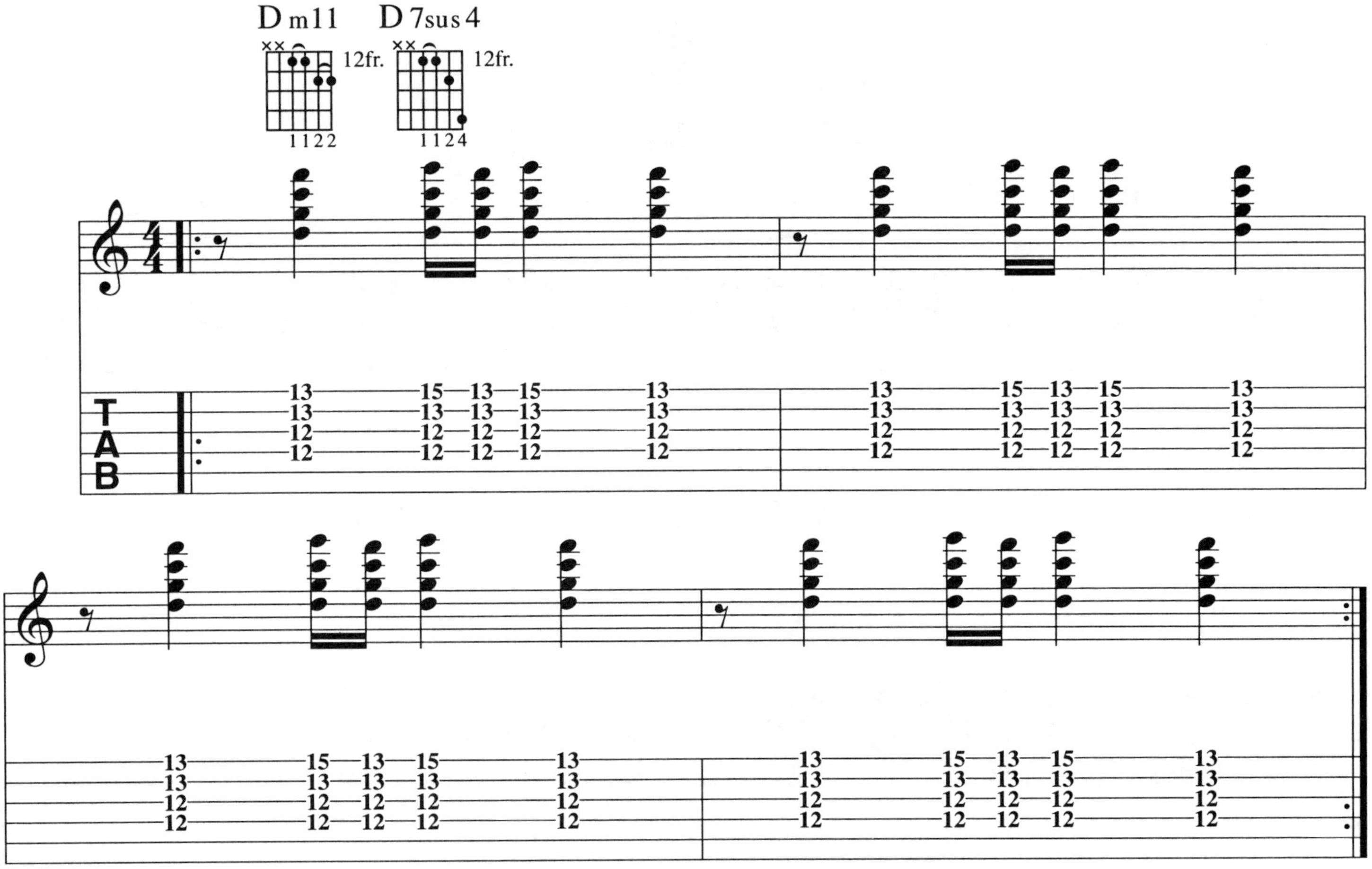

Dm11 D7sus4

12fr. 12fr.

1122 1124

This example is in the style of the S.O.S. Band.

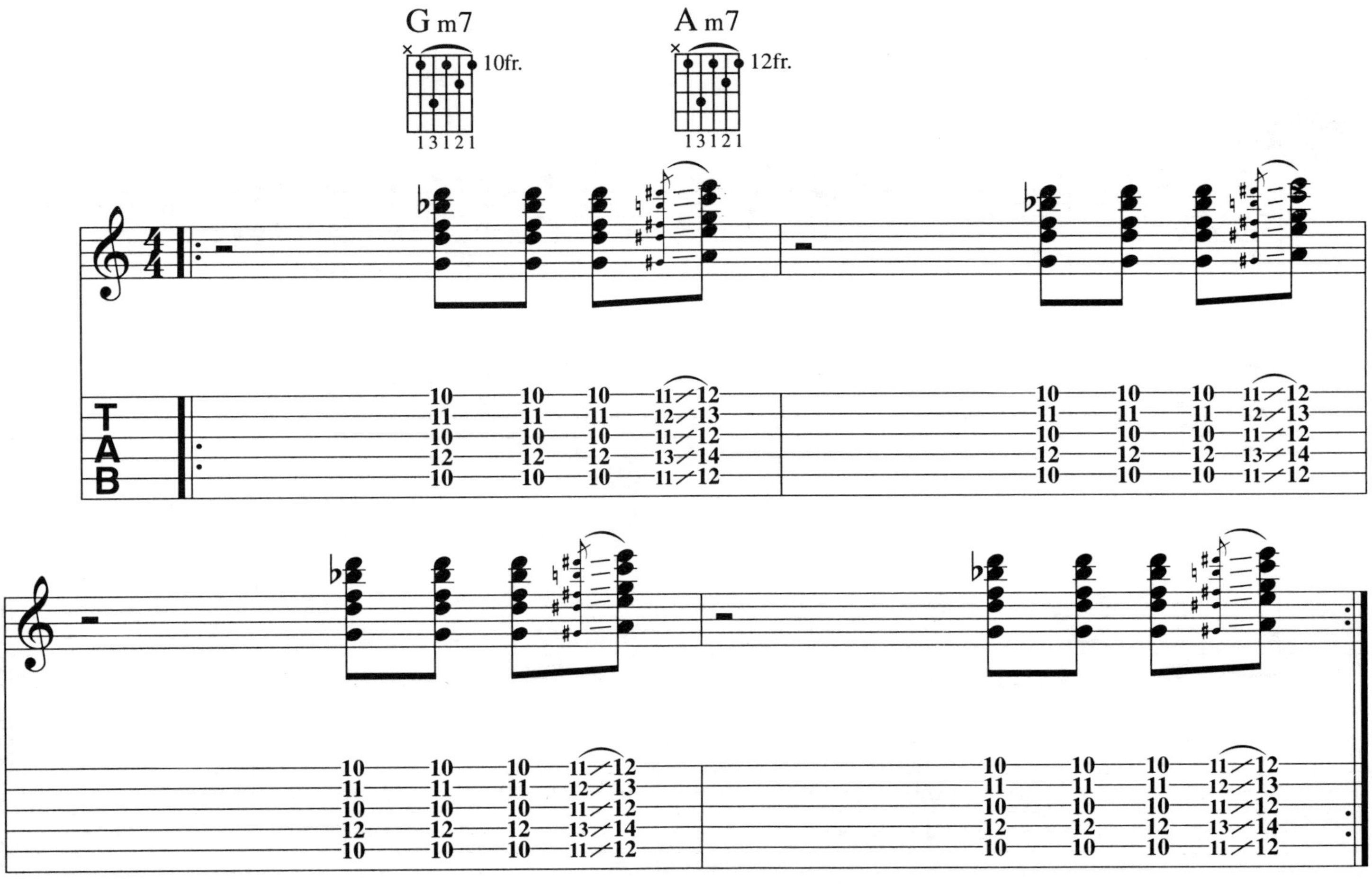

Gm7 Am7

10fr. 12fr.

13121 13121

This example is in the style of Brick.

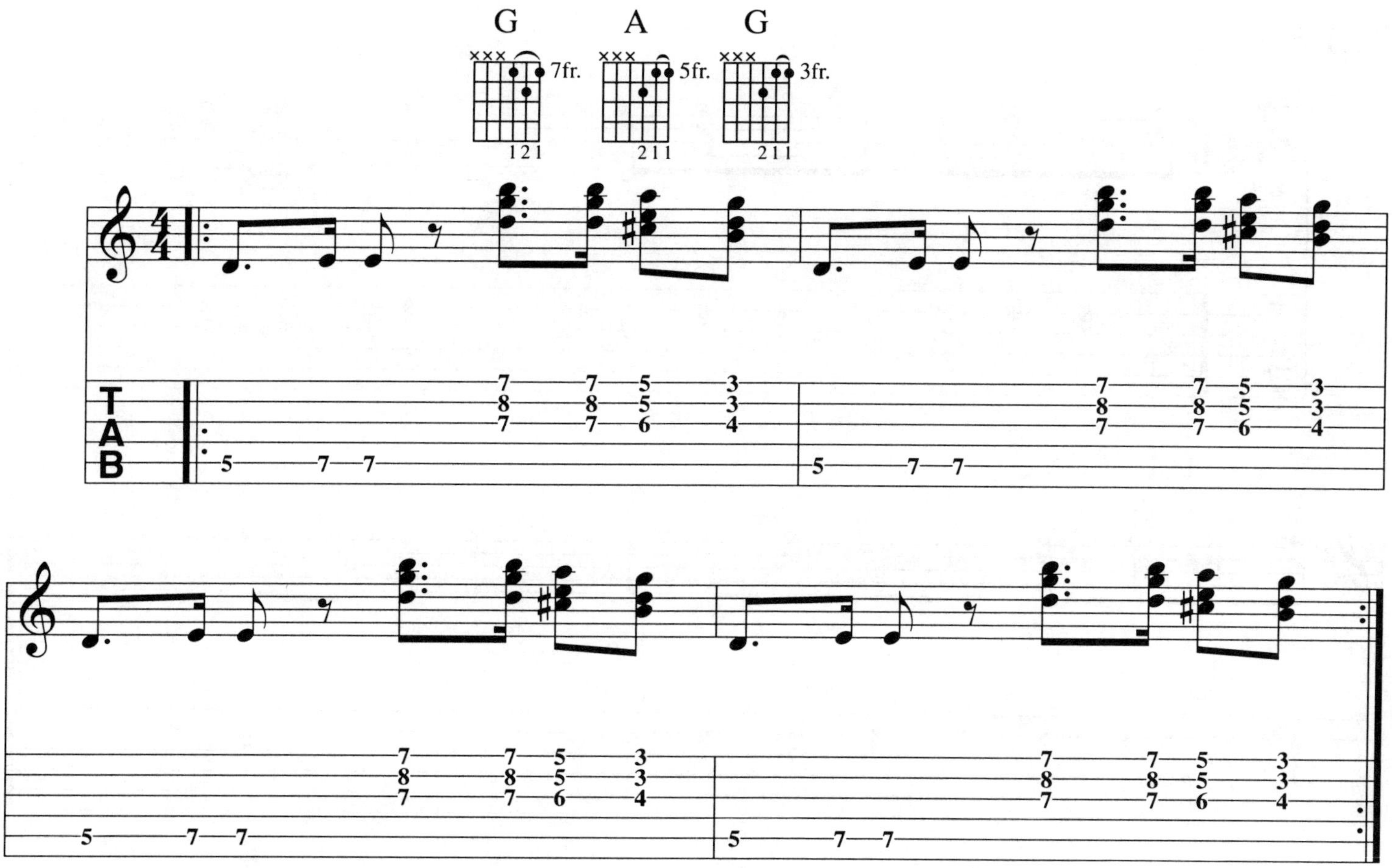

G
A
G
7fr.
5fr.
3fr.
TAB

This example is in the style of Lakeside.

G
F
12fr.
10fr.
TAB

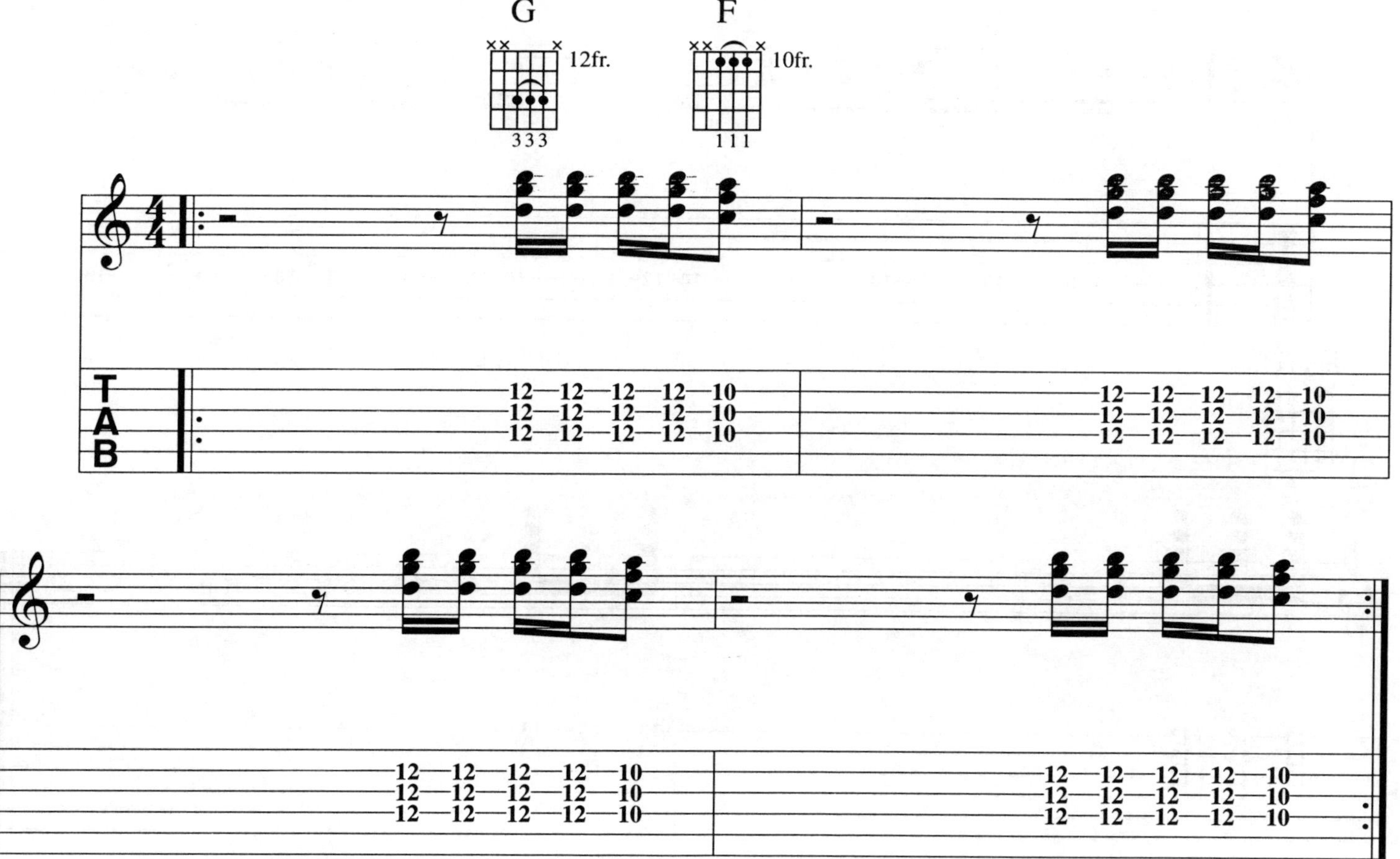

This example is in the style of P-Funk.

This example is in the style of Taste of Honey.

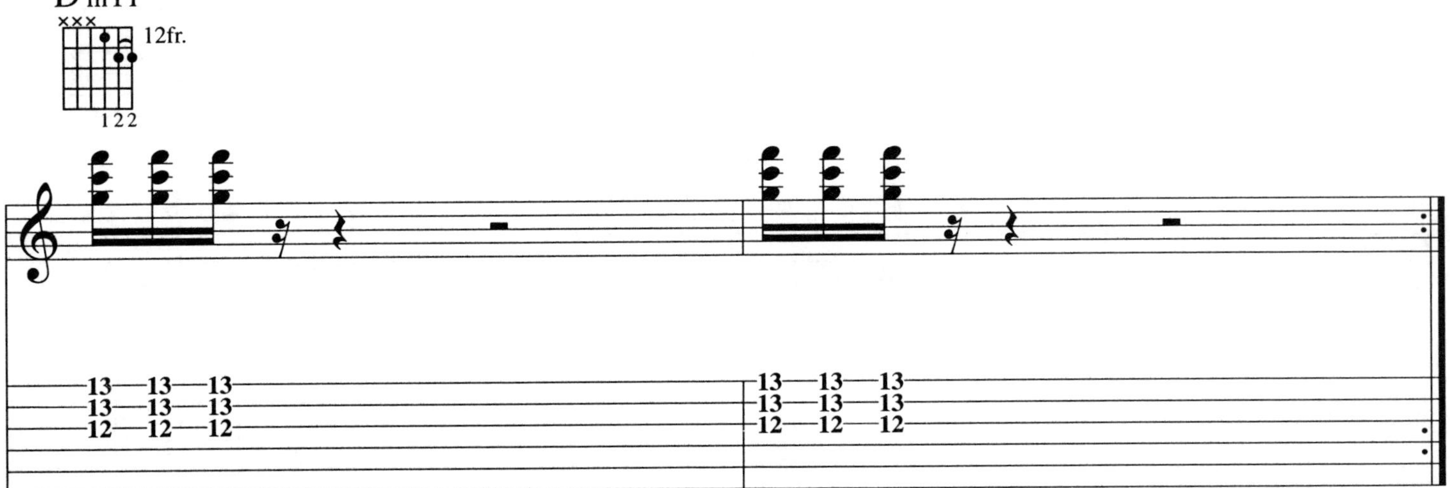

This example is in the style of the Ohio Players.

This example is in the style of Stevie Wonder.

This example is in the style of the Dazz Band.

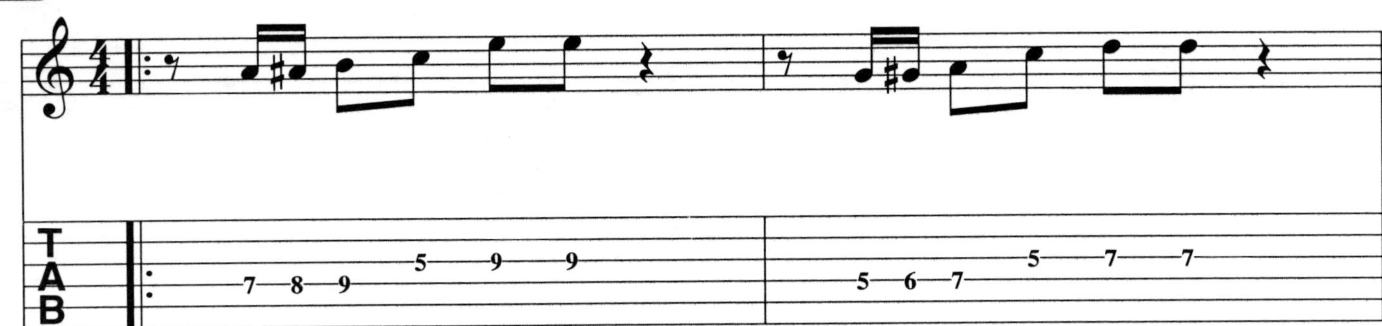

This example is in the style of Con Funk Shun.

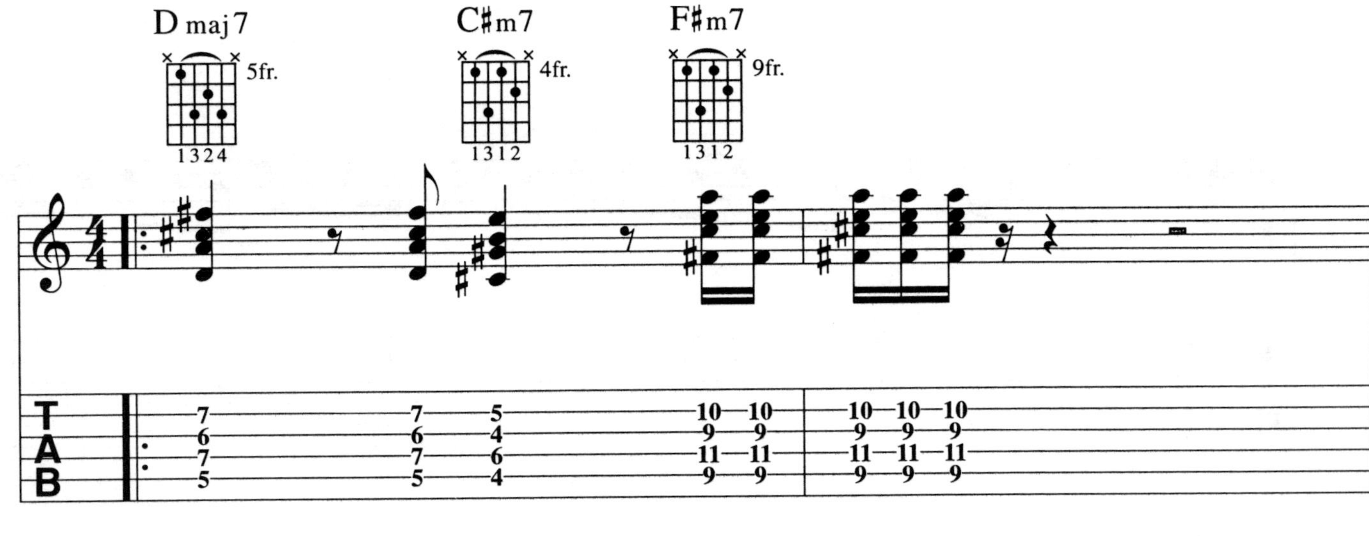

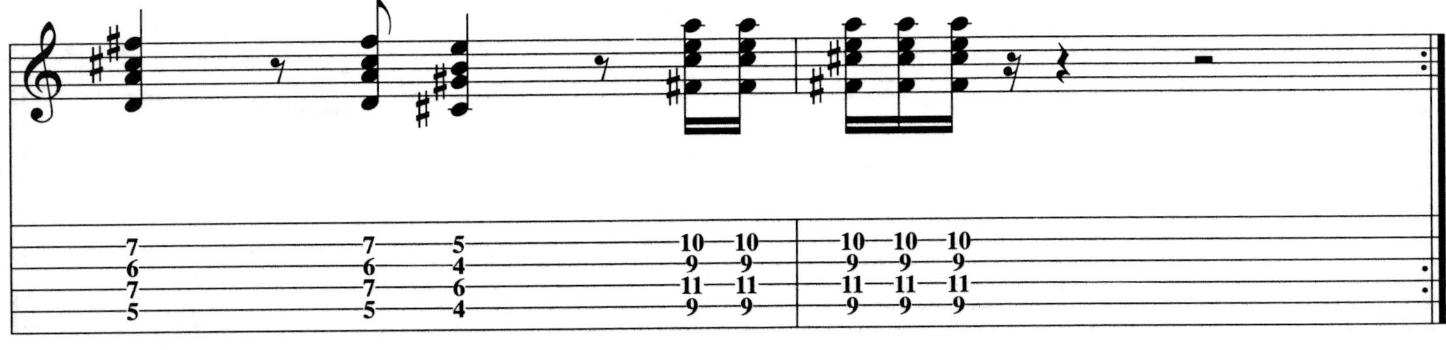

These next two examples are in the style of Michael Jackson.

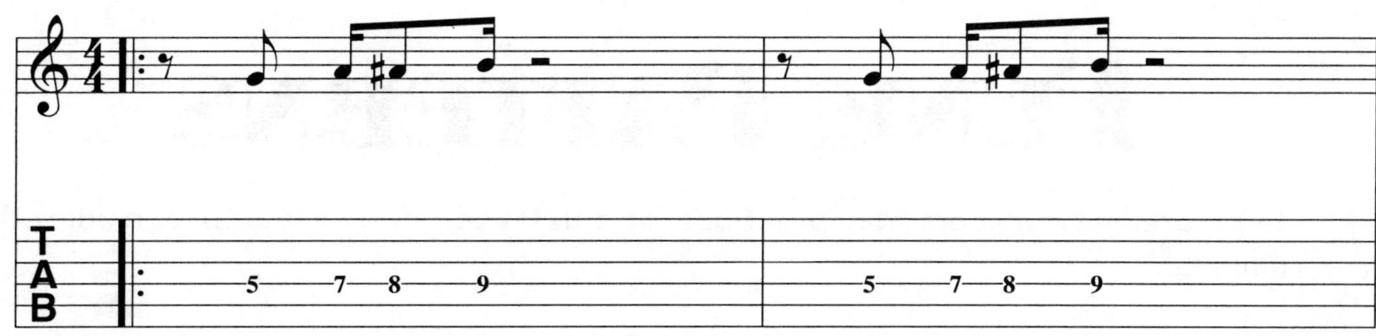

CREATING SINGLE-LINE FUNK PATTERNS

There are several common practices of this type. We have to consider these important intervals.

These two notes are ***enharmonic*** which means they sound the same pitch but have different names..

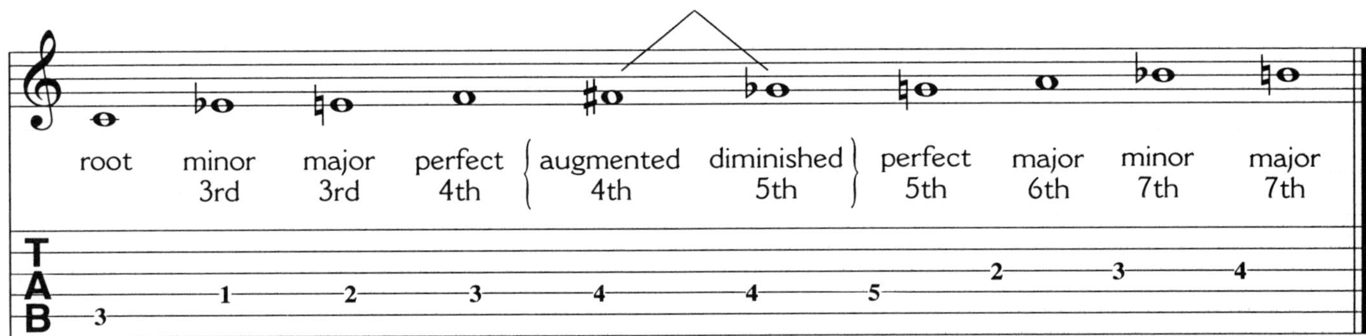

What we will attempt to do in the following examples is to use a simple basic rhythm to highlight the pitches commonly used. Remember most patterns recur every measure, every two measures or every four measures.

We will start simply with two-note ascending patterns.

The use of the ***major 6th*** and the ***minor 7th*** of the key either alone and/or the use of a passing tone such as the minor 7th in the case of the 6th is often used.

Another common pattern is the ***minor 7th*** to ***root*** movement.

The next examples show some possible variations.

The number of possible variations increases exponentially with the number of notes in the pattern.

MELODIC REVERSE = The pitch order is reversed but rhythmic order is ***static*** (same).

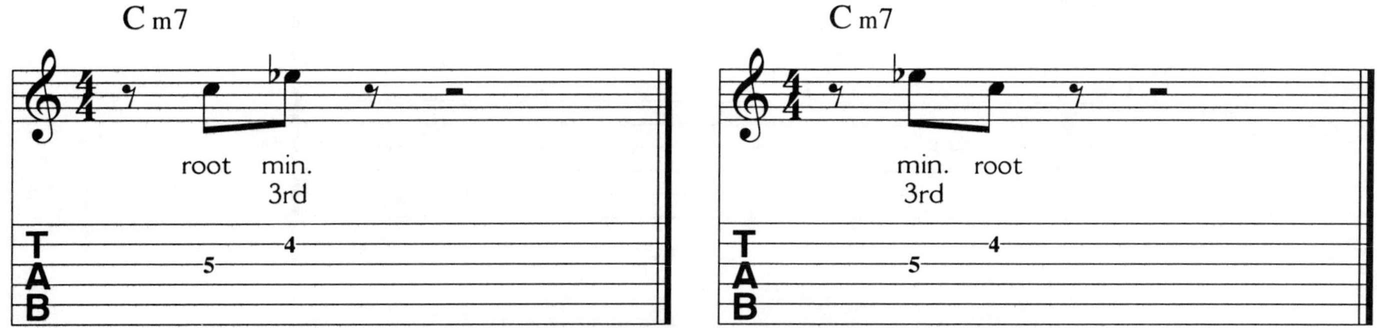

RHYTHMIC INVERSION = The rhythymic order is reversed within the measure but the pitch order is static.

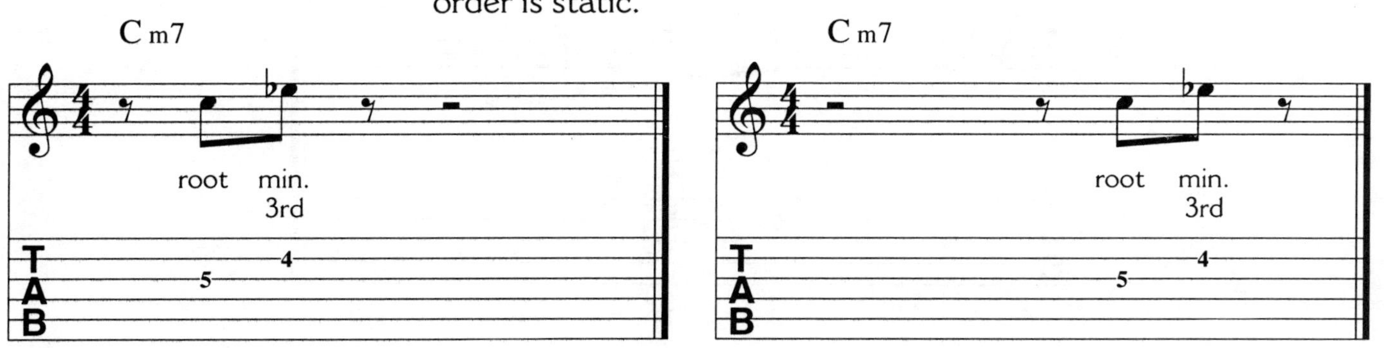

MELODIC REVERSE AND RHYTHMIC INVERSION = The melodic order is reversed and rhythmic order is inverted.

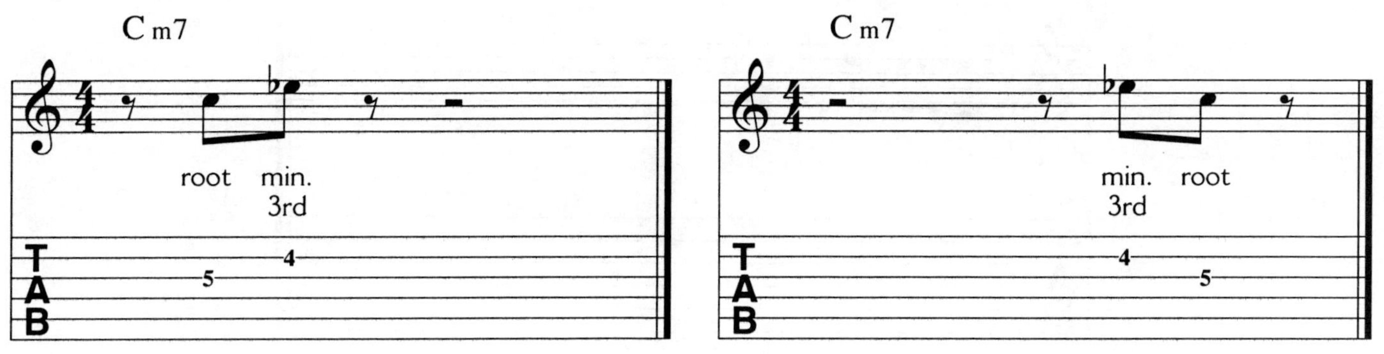

Base Pattern

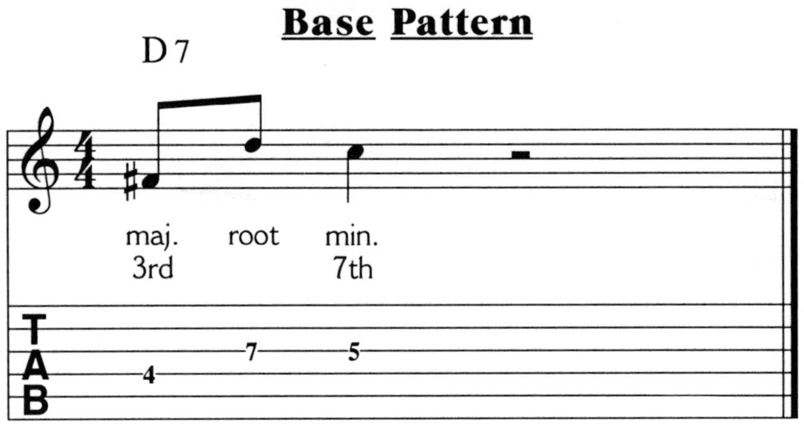

Melodic Reverse

Rhythmic Reverse

Melodic Inversion

Rhythmic Inversion

Melodic and Rhythmic Reverse

Base Pattern and Rhythmic Inversion

Rhythmic Inversion and Base Pattern

Base Pattern

Melodic Reverse

Rhythmic Reverse and Melodic

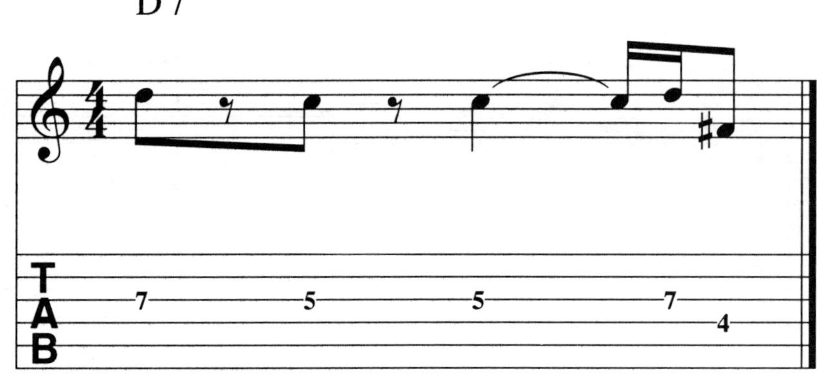

Rhythmic Reverse

☆☆☆

CREATING CHORD PATTERNS

Creating chord patterns using the permutation concept previously shown only involves the rhythm variations. To help you get the feel of this chordal syncopation, let's start with the classic "Hambone" rhythm.

Here are a few examples of variations that could derive from any pattern.

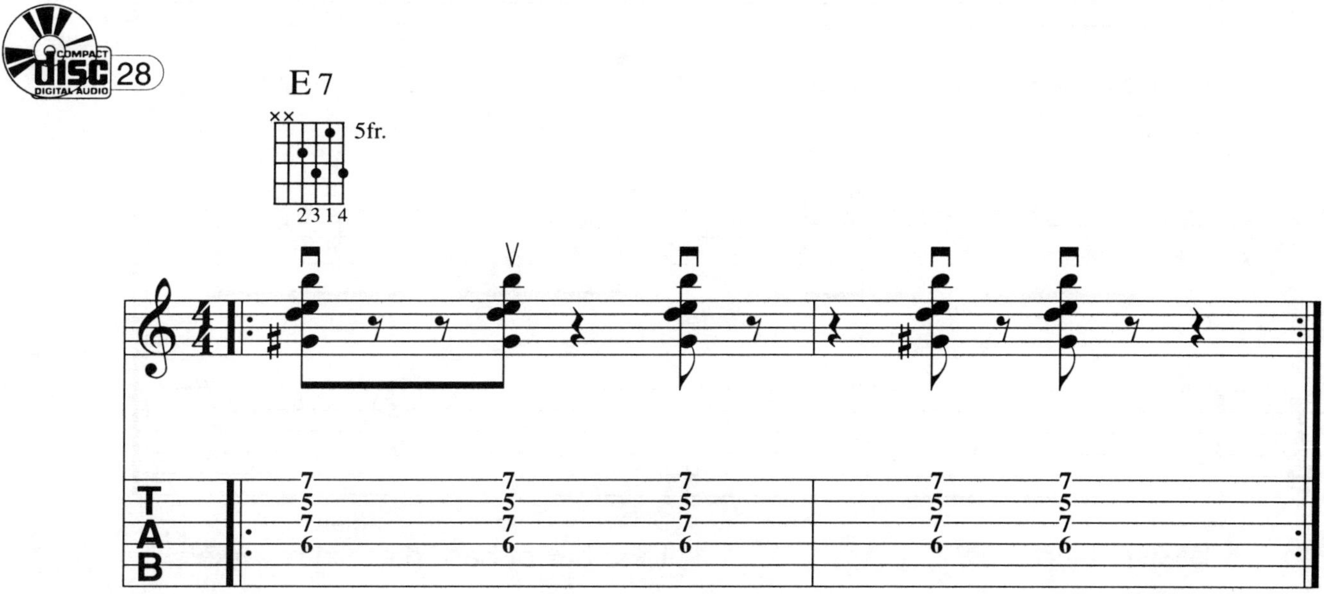

Same pattern in the constant eighth-note stroke style. Note: x type noteheads indicate finger-board hand dampening where the finger board hand does not apply enough pressure for the chord to fully sound.

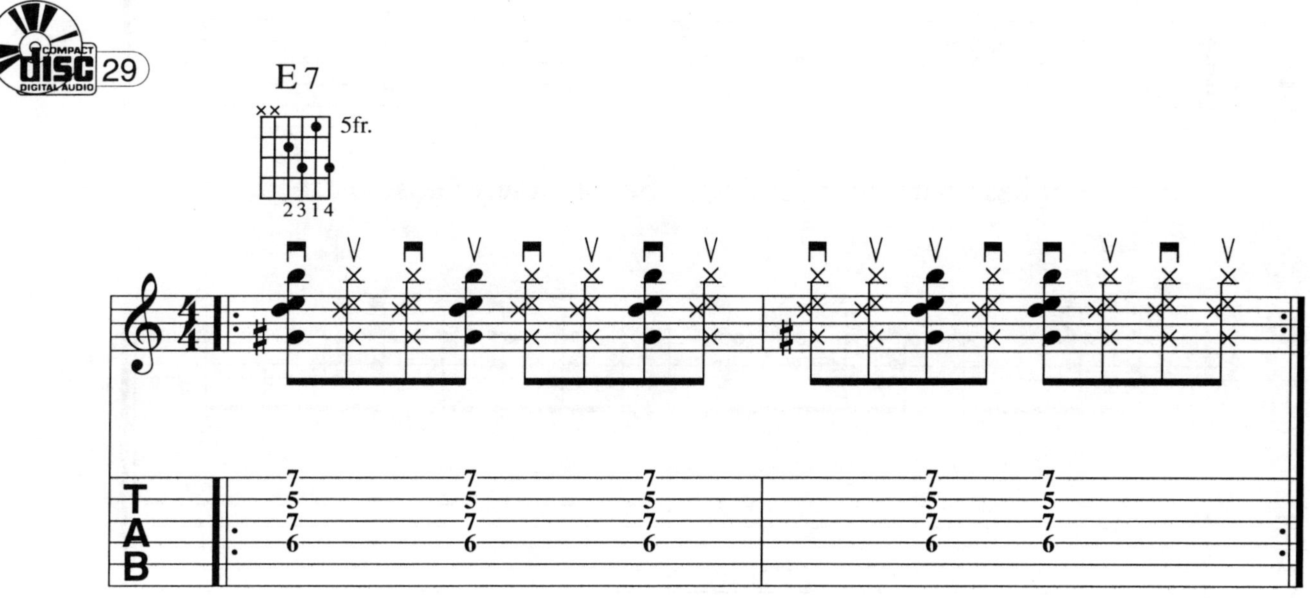

Rhythmic Variations

First bar of base pattern reversed (partial reverse)

Second bar of base pattern reversed (partial reverse)

30

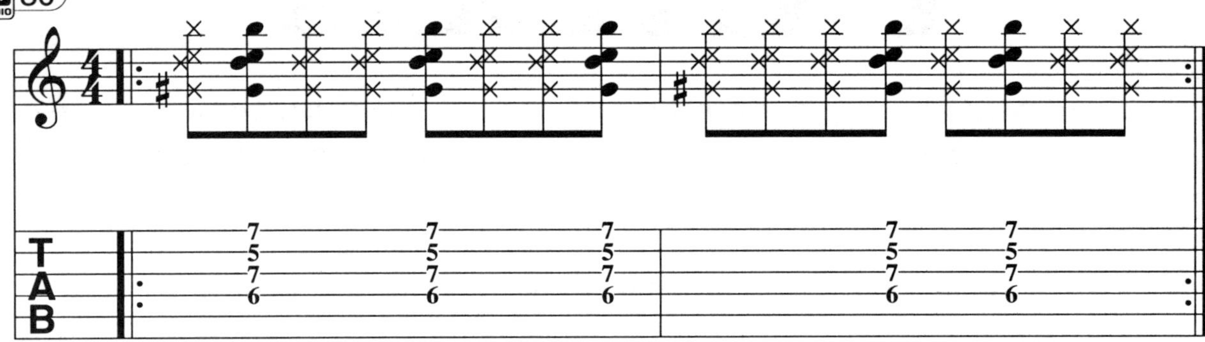

Entire base pattern reversed

31

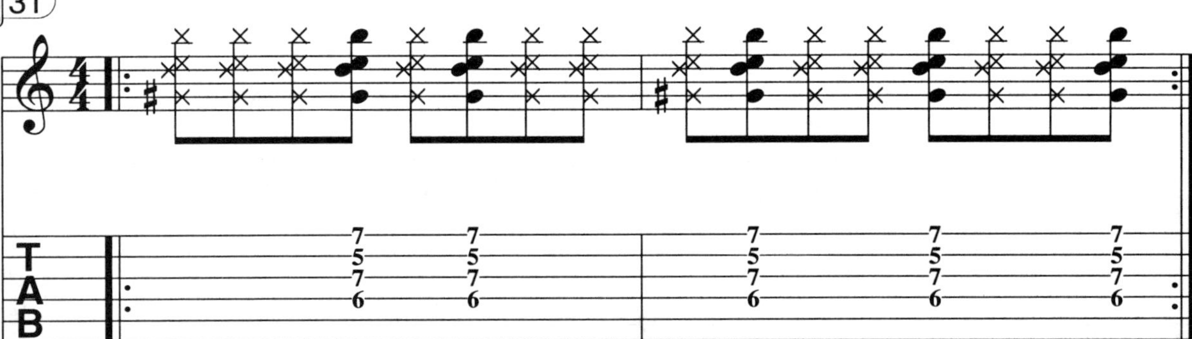

Base pattern

First bar of base pattern reversed

32

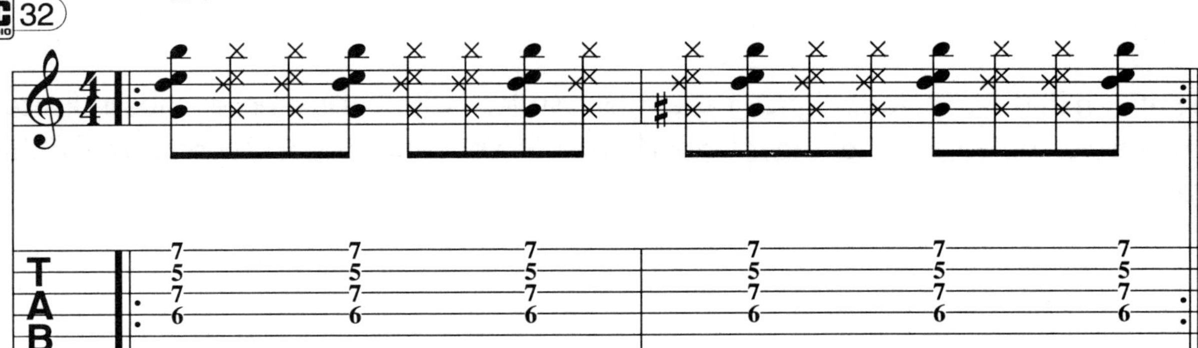

First bar of base pattern reversed

Second bar of base pattern

33

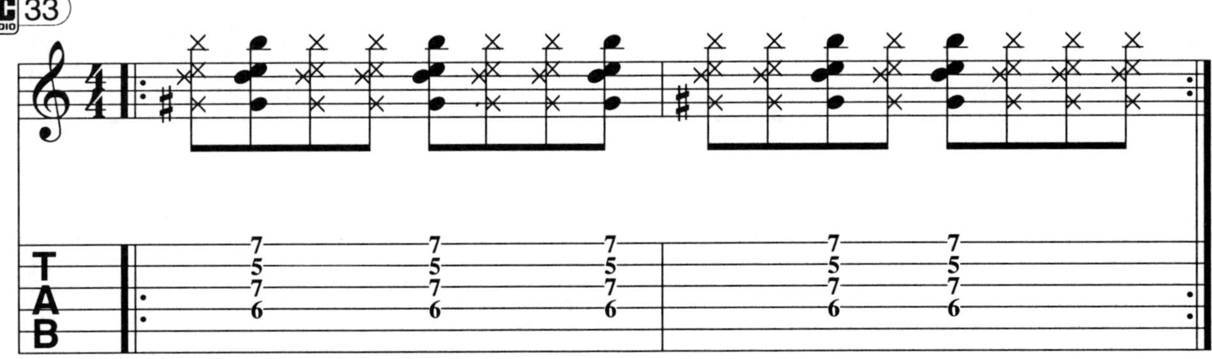

Combination of base pattern alternating with the base pattern reversed.

Base pattern

E 7

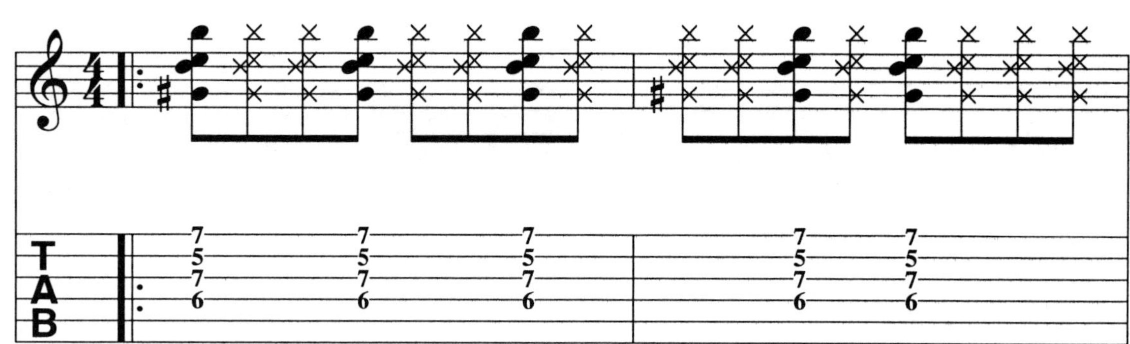

First bar of base pattern
partially reversed

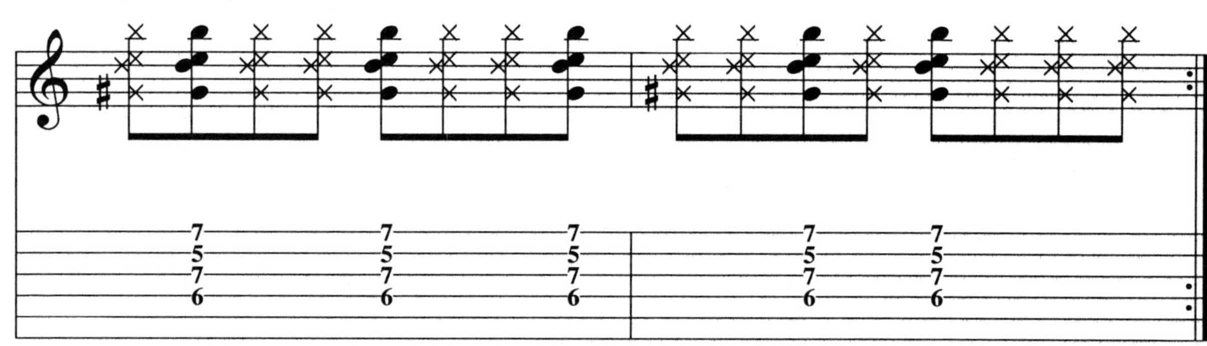

Base pattern

E 7

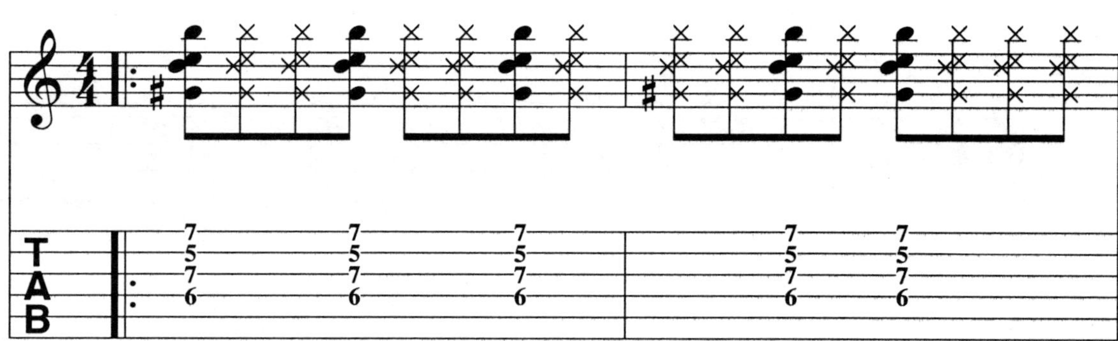

Second bar of base pattern
partially reversed

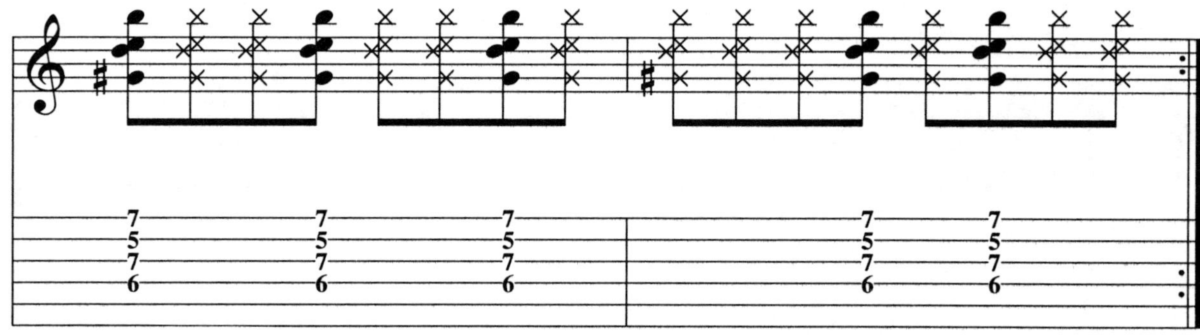

☆☆

Etudes

01

These patterns are just suggestions, try creating your own also.

02

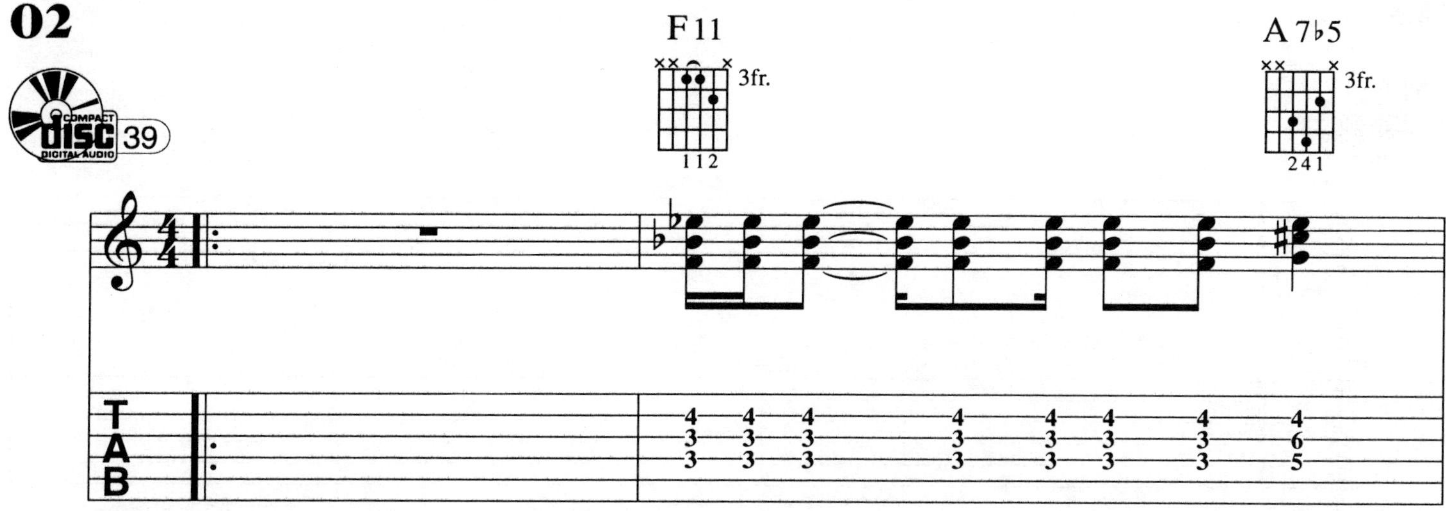

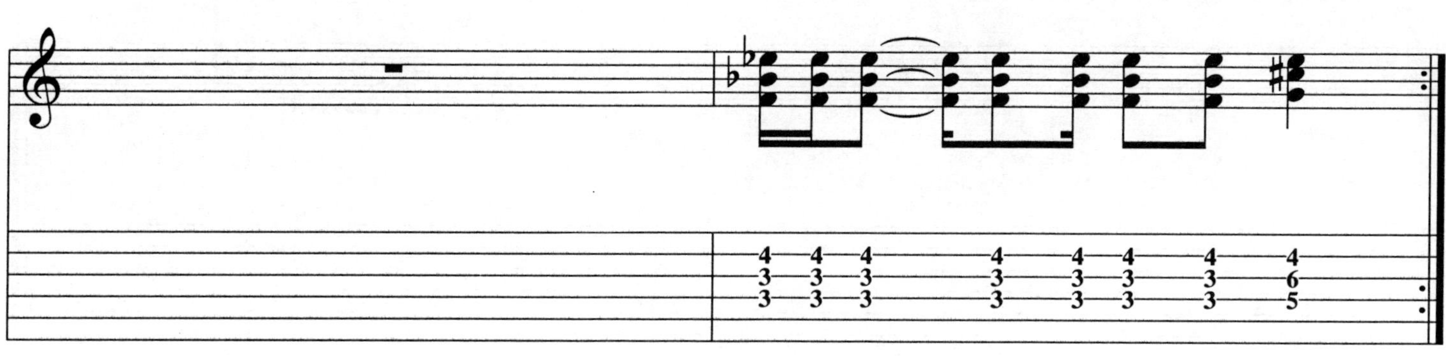

03

40

C 6 3fr. 111

C 9 3fr. 111

C 7♯9 2fr. 2134

TAB

C 6 C 9 C 7♯9

04

41

TAB

05

42

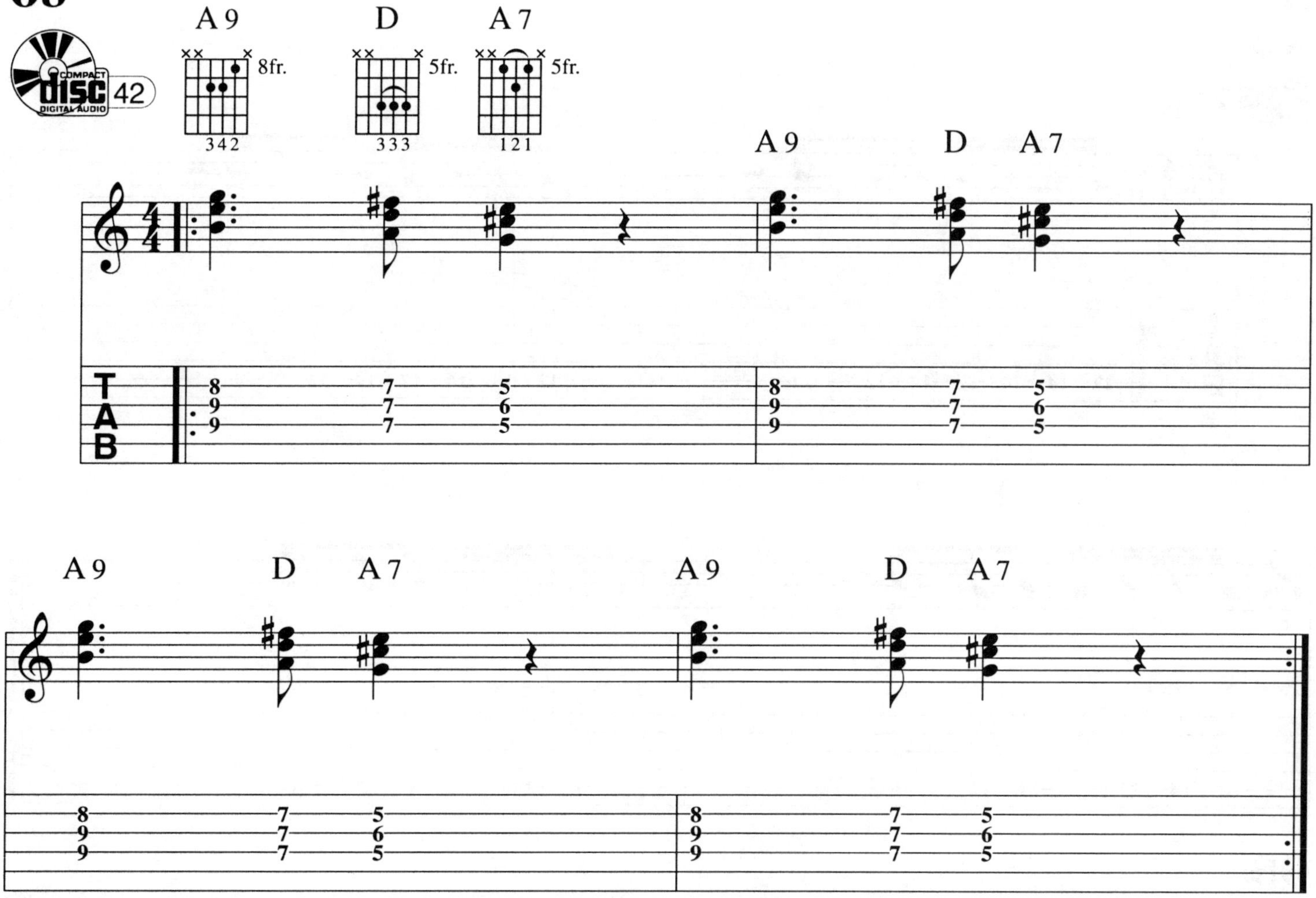

A 9 — 8fr. — 342

D — 5fr. — 333

A 7 — 5fr. — 121

A 9 D A 7

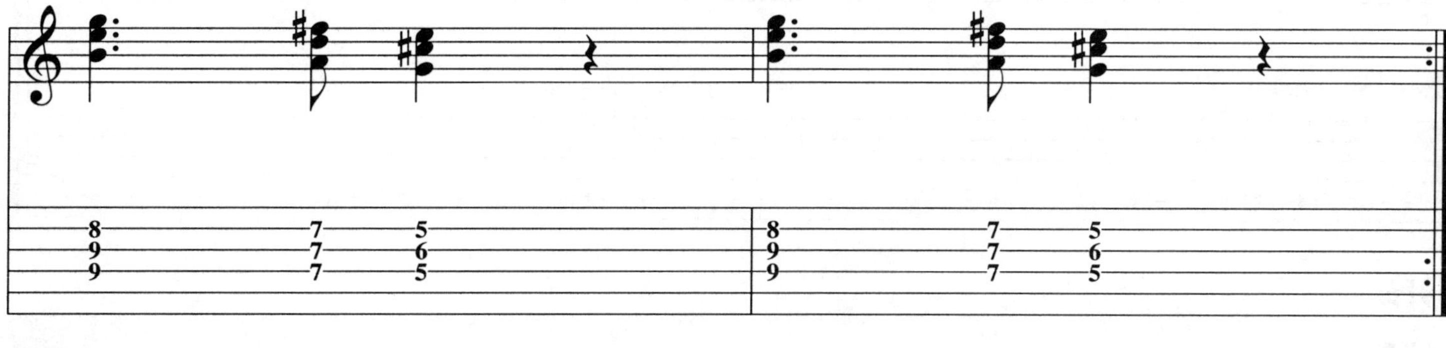

07

COMPACT
disc
DIGITAL AUDIO
44

08

COMPACT
disc
DIGITAL AUDIO
45
A 7sus 4
5fr.
1 3 1
A 7
5fr.
1 2 1

A 7sus 4
A 7

09

COMPACT
disc
DIGITAL AUDIO
46

10

COMPACT
disc
DIGITAL AUDIO
47

11

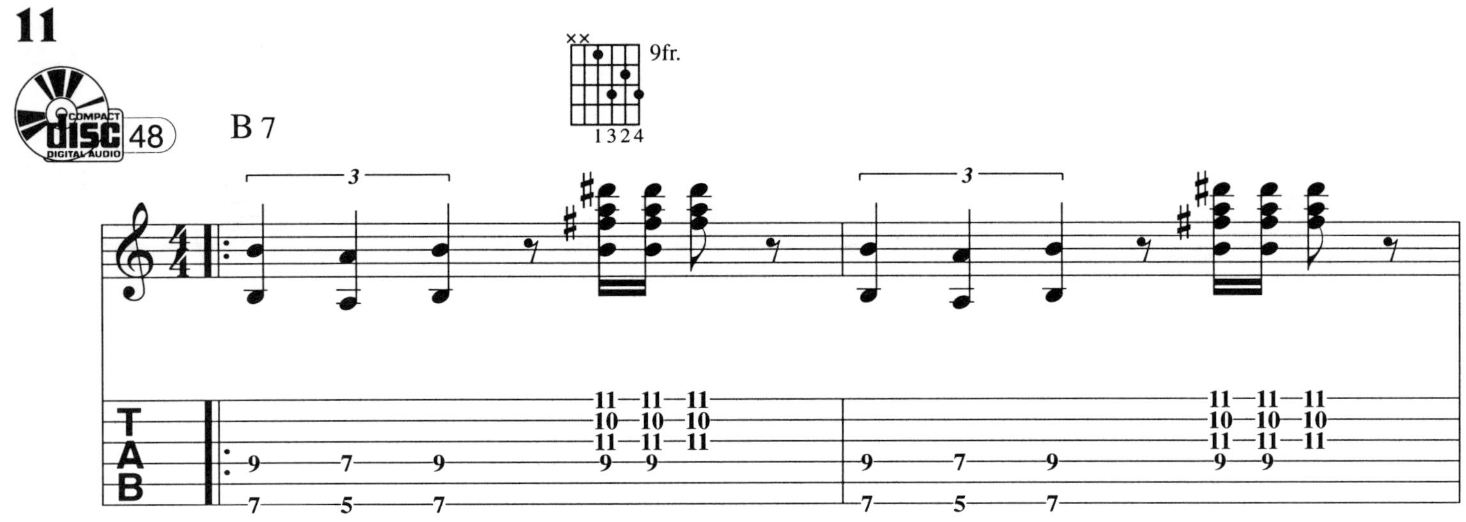

12

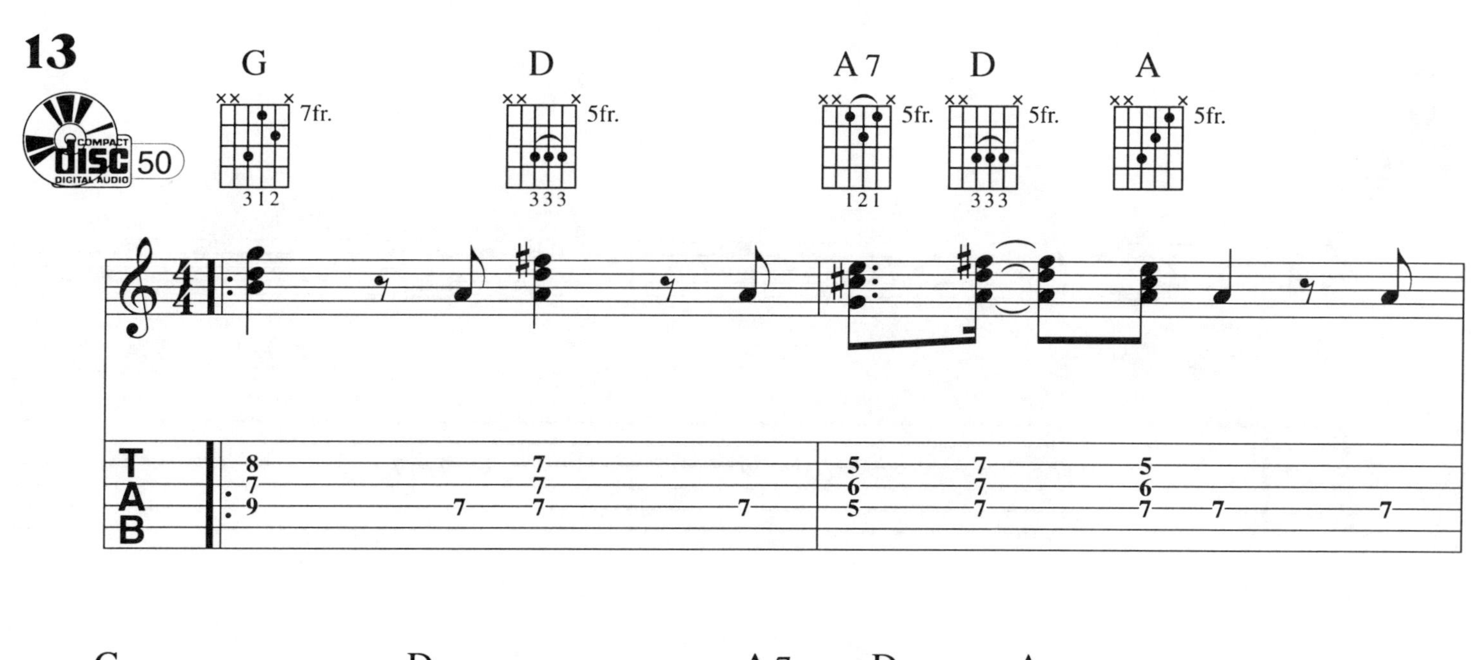

14

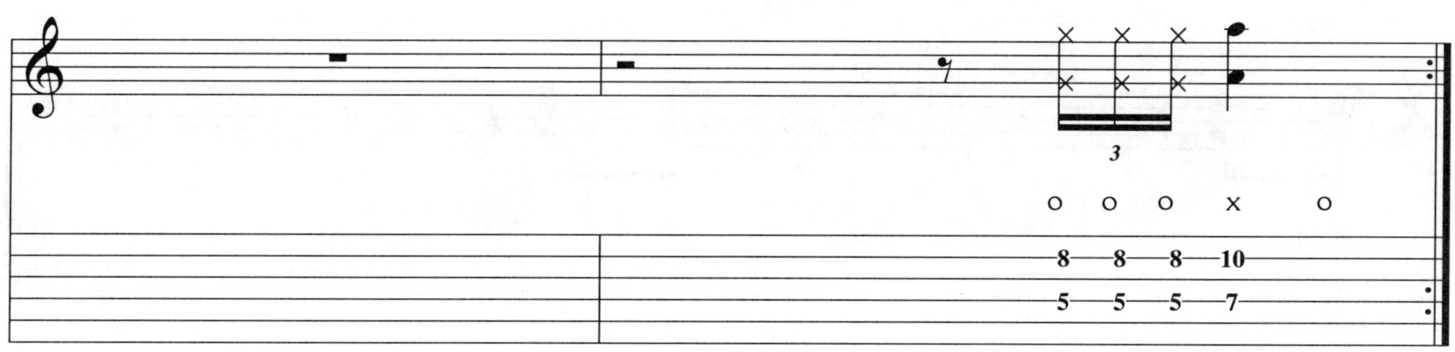

15

COMPACT
disc
DIGITAL AUDIO
52

T
A
B
7 7 7 7 7 9
7 7 7 7 7 9

10 10 9 9 10 9
10 10 9 9 10 9

16

COMPACT
disc
DIGITAL AUDIO
53

T
A
B

COMPACT
disc
DIGITAL AUDIO
54

18

COMPACT
disc
DIGITAL AUDIO
55

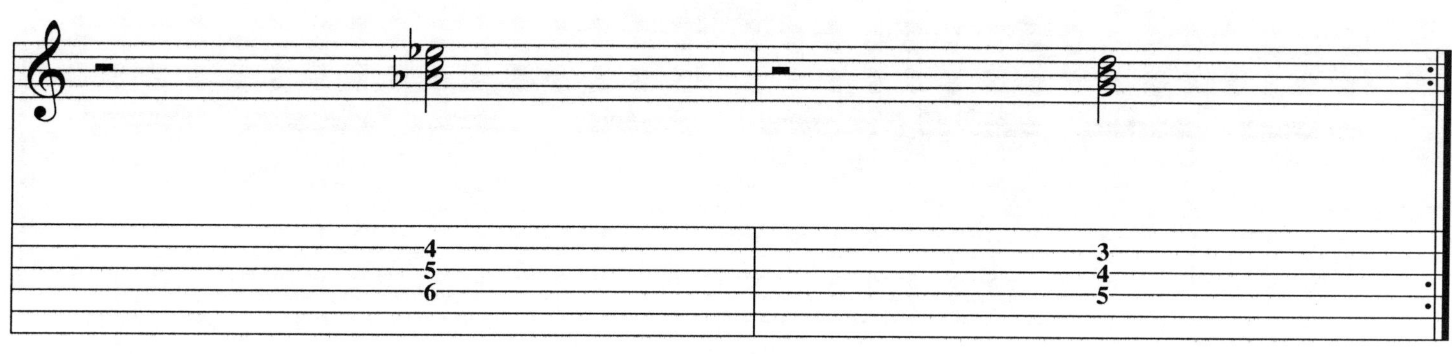

19

20

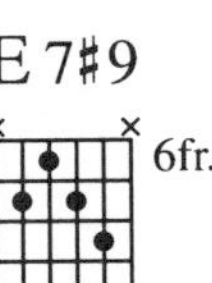

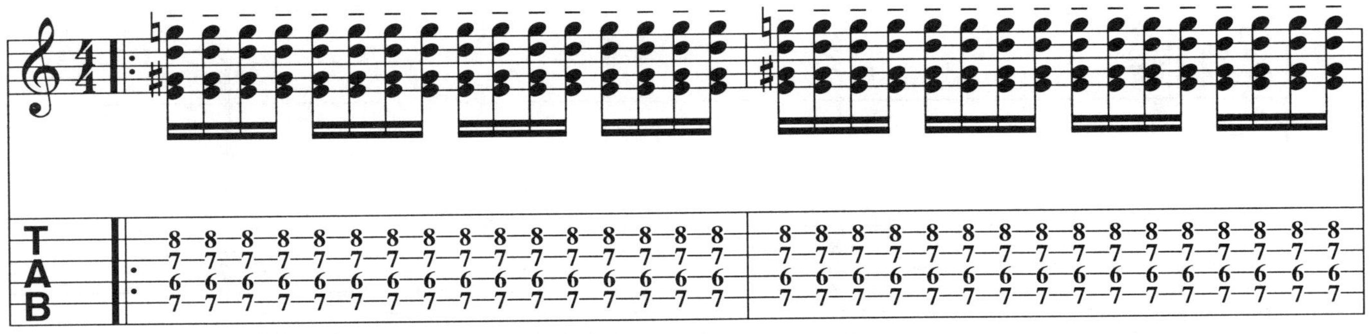

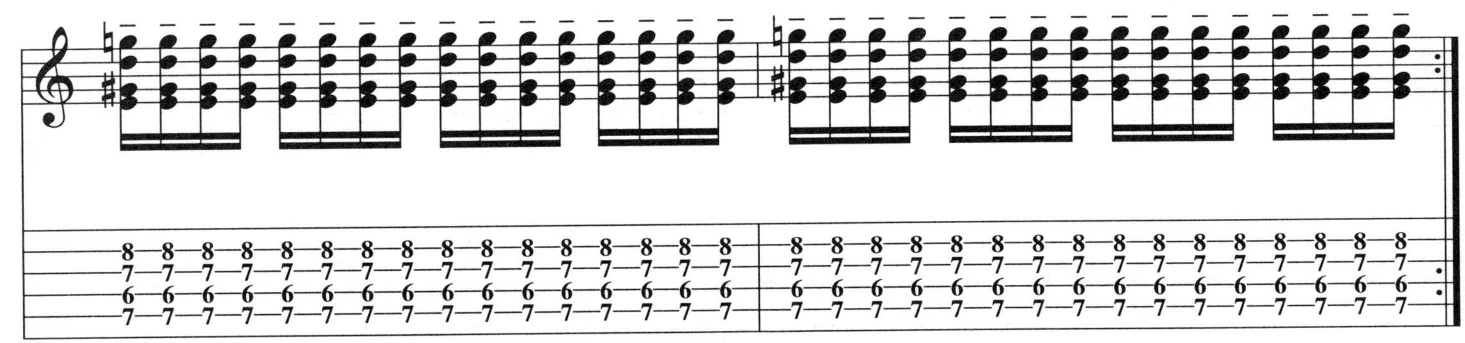

21

58
T
A
B
7 7 7 7 7 7 7 7

7 7 7 7 7 7 7 5 7 7 5

22

59
D 7
5fr.
314
D 7sus 4
5fr.
314
T
A
B

D 7sus 4
D 7

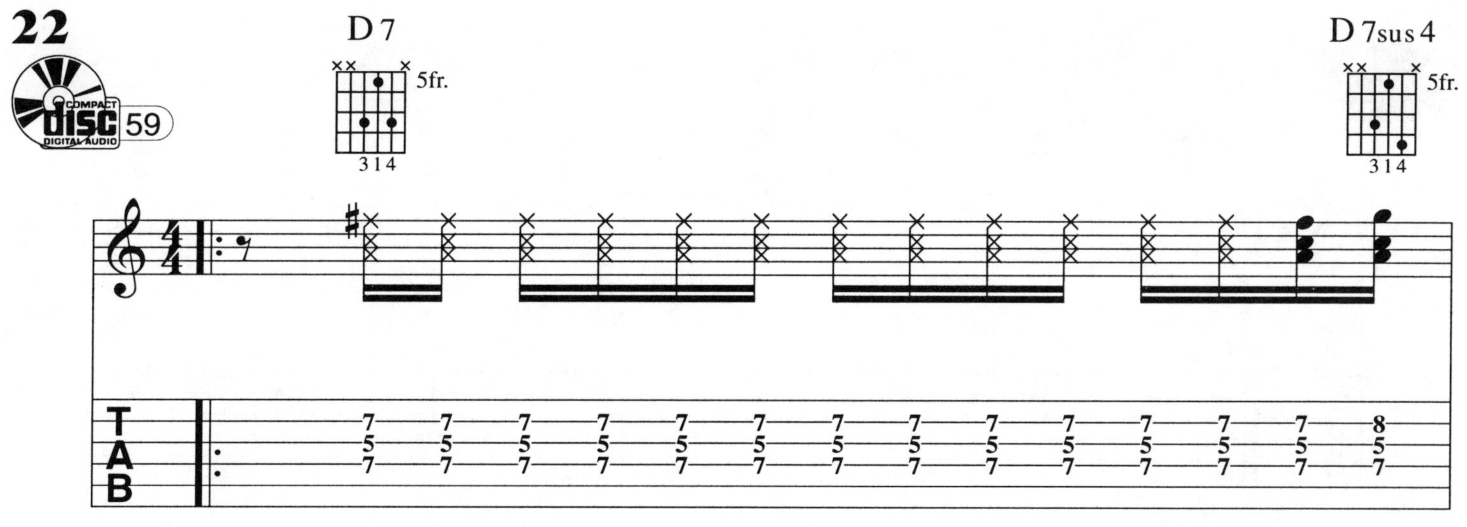

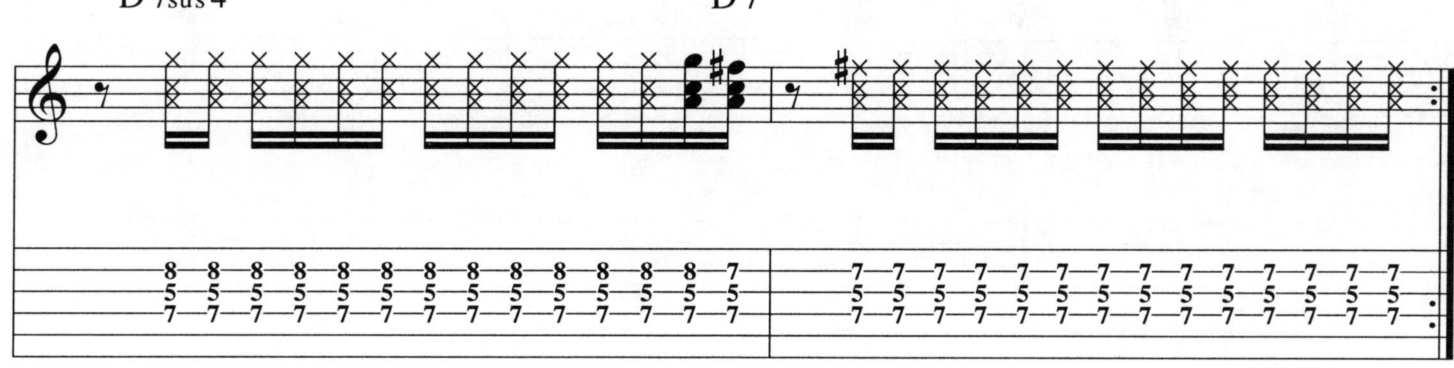

23

24

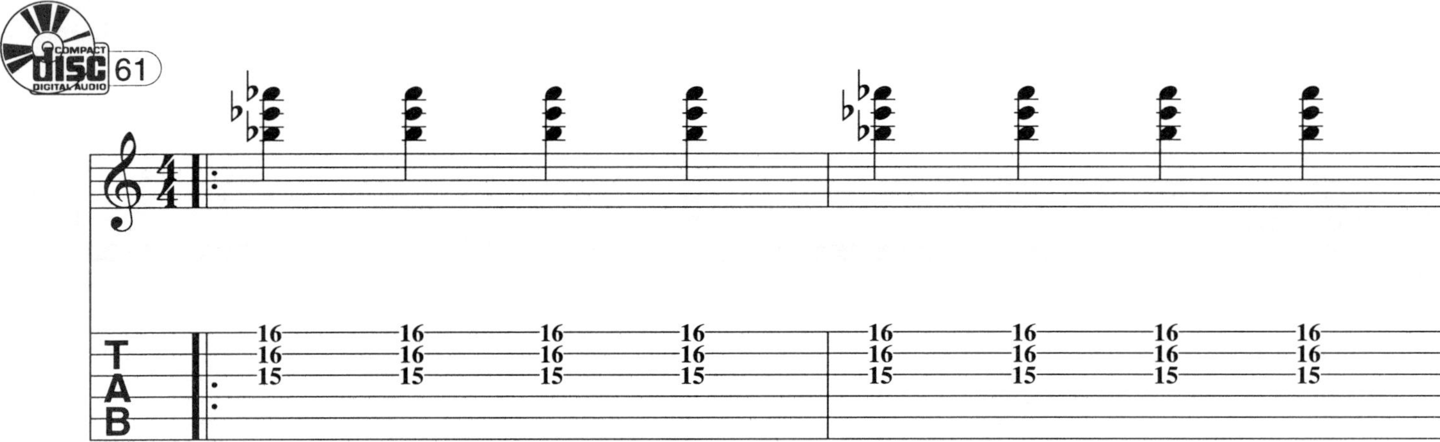

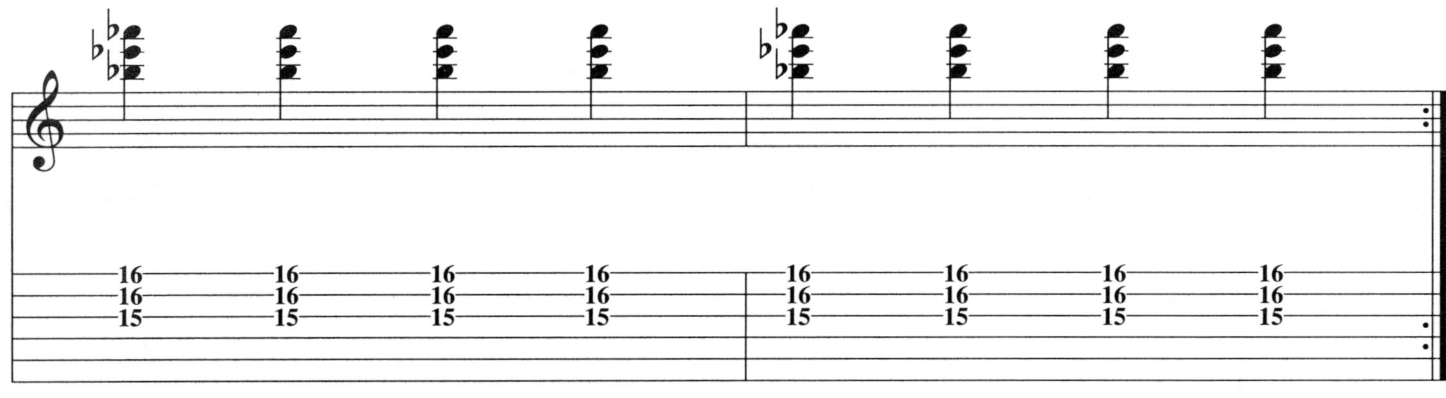

25

26

COMPACT disc DIGITAL AUDIO 63

27

64

28

65

☆☆

Common Funk Chords

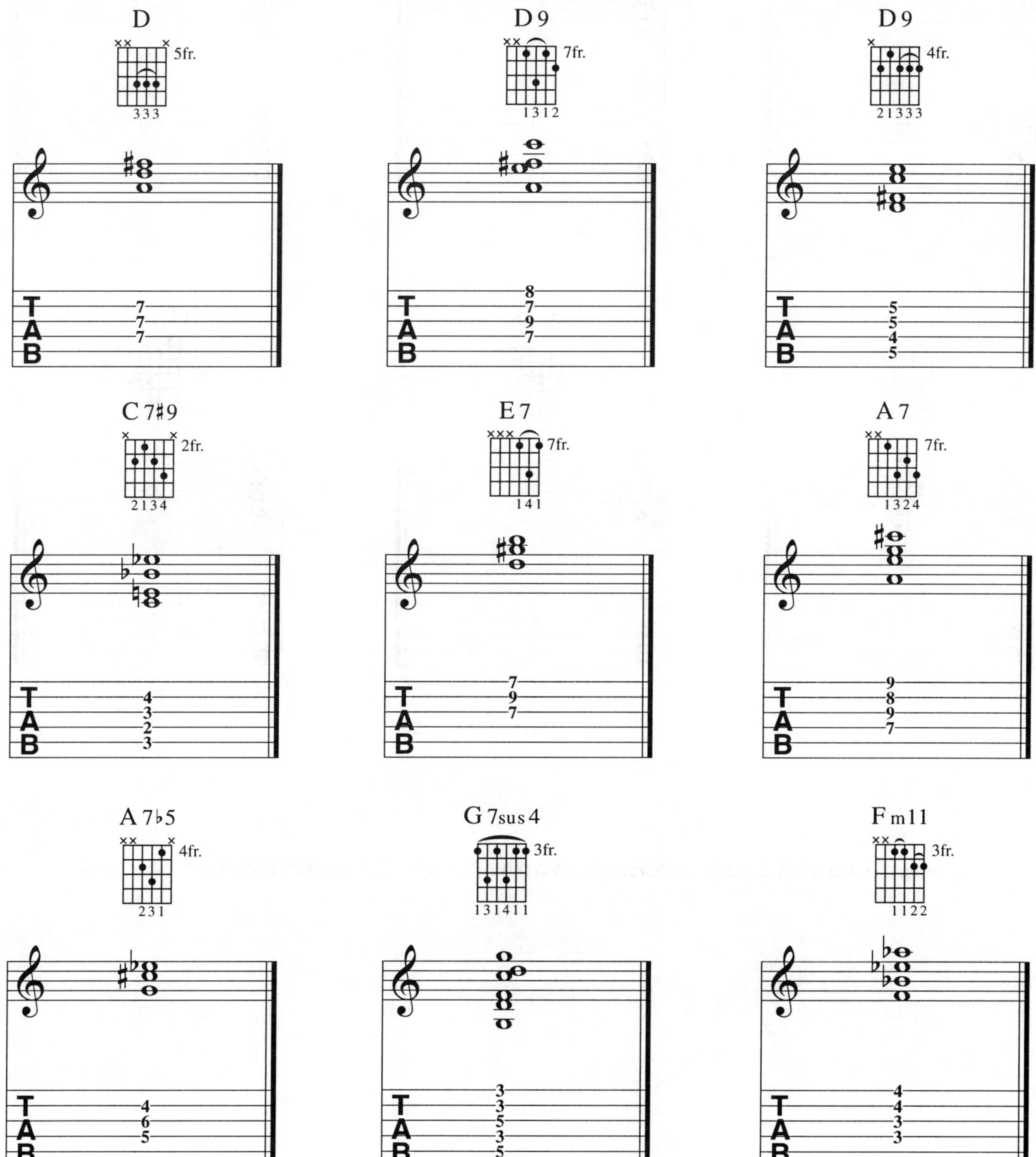

E 7sus 4
7fr.
141
G sus
3fr.
311
C m7
3fr.
13121
7
10
7
3
3
5
3
4
3
5
3
G m7
3fr.
131111
A m6
5fr.
314
G maj 7
5fr.
1333
3
3
3
3
5
3
7
5
7
7
7
7
5

☆☆

DISCOGRAPHY

AVERAGE WHITE BAND

1984	Best of Average White Band	RCA
1997	Pick Up the Pieces & Other Hits	Rhino
1998	The Very Best of Average White Band	Music Club
1998	Classic Cuts	Snapper

B.T. EXPRESS

1974	Do It	Roadshow
1975	Non-Stop	Roadshow
1976	Energy	Columbia
1977	Function at the Junction	Columbia

BAR-KAYS

1967	Soul Finger	Rhino
1976	Too Hot to Stop	Mercury

BRASS CONSTRUCTION

1975	Brass Construction	United Artists
1976	Brass Construction 2	United Artists

BRICK

2002	The Essentials	Rhino
1995	The Best of Brick	Epic/Bang
2000	Super Hits	Sony

JAMES BROWN

1965	Papa's Got a Brand New Bag	Polygram
1967	Cold Sweat	King

Cameo

1984 She's Strange	Casablanca
1986 Word Up	Mercury

Commodores

1974 Machine Gun	Motown
1975 Caught in the Act	Motown
1975 Movin' On	Motown
1976 Hot on the Tracks	Motown

Earth Wind and Fire

1970 Earth Wind and Fire	Warner Bros.
1971 The Need of Love	Warner Bros.
1972 Last Days and Time	Columbia
1973 Head to the Sky	Columbia

The Gap Band

1974 Magician's Holiday	Shelter
1976 The Gap Band (Tattoo)	Tattoo
1979 The Gap Band II	Mercury
1980 The Gap Band III	Mercury

Isley Brothers

1969 The Brothers Isley	T-Neck
1975 The Heat is On	T-Neck

Michael Jackson

1979 Off the Wall	Epic
1982 Thriller	Epic

Parliament-Funkadelics

1974 Up for the Downstroke	Casablanca
1976 Mothership Connection	Casablanca

Prince

1979 Prince	Warner Bros.
1987 Sign o' the Times	Paisley Park

Sly and the Family Stone

1969 Stand!	Epic
1973 Fresh	Epic

Tower of Power

1973 Tower of Power	Warner Bros.
1974 Back to Oakland	Warner Bros.

War

1971 All Day Music	Rhino
1972 The World is a Ghetto	Rhino

Stevie Wonder

1972 Music of My Mind	Motown
1973 Innervisions	Motown

☆☆☆

APPENDIX

C
3 2 1
T
A
B
0
1
0
2
3

C
3fr.
1 3 3 3
T
A
B
5
5
5
3

C
8fr.
1 3 4 2 1 1
T
A
B
8
8
9
10
10
8

C
8fr.
3 2 1 1
T
A
B
8
8
9
10

C
5fr.
1 1 1
T
A
B
5
5
5

C
5fr.
4 3 1 1 1
T
A
B
5
5
5
7
8

C6
4 3 2 1
T
A
B
1
2
2
3

C6
10fr.
1 3 2 4
T
A
B
12
10
12
10

C6
2fr.
2 1 1 4
T
A
B
5
2
2
3

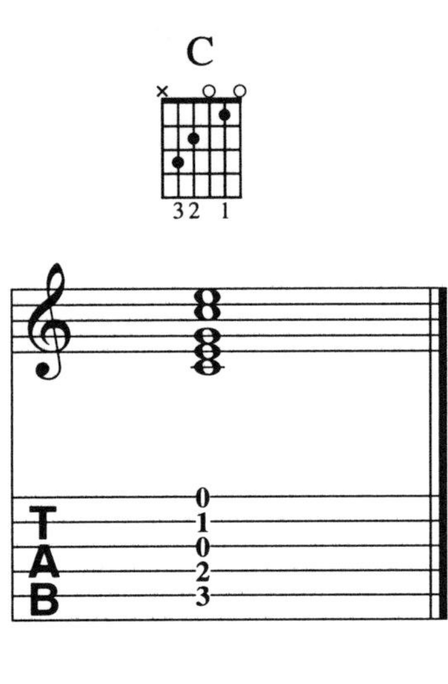

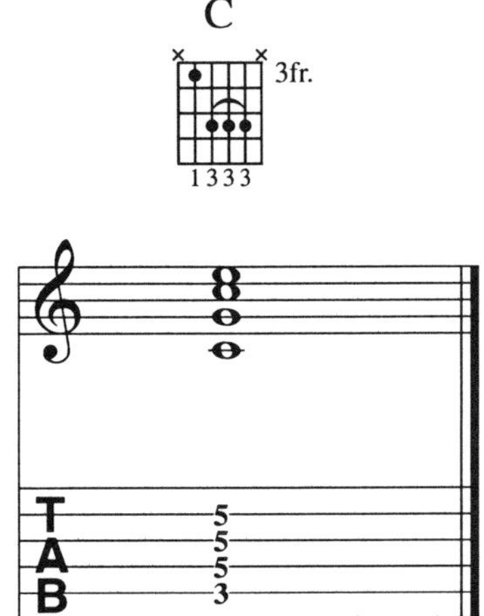

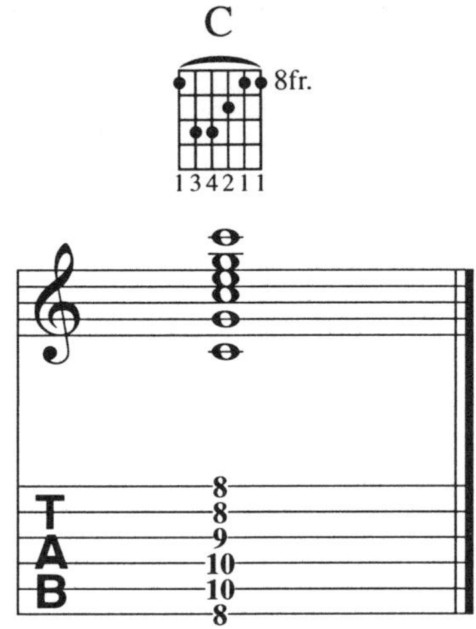

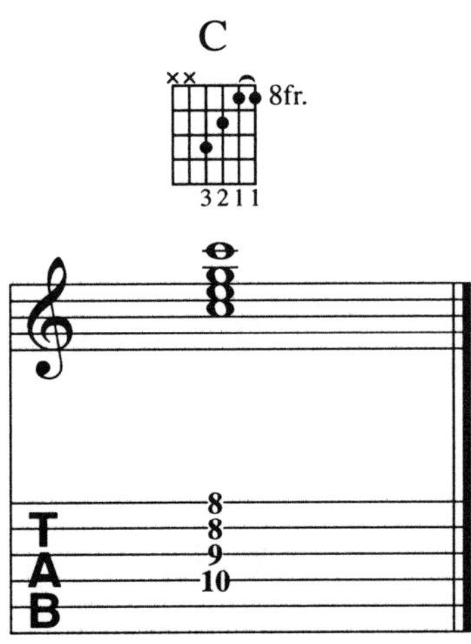

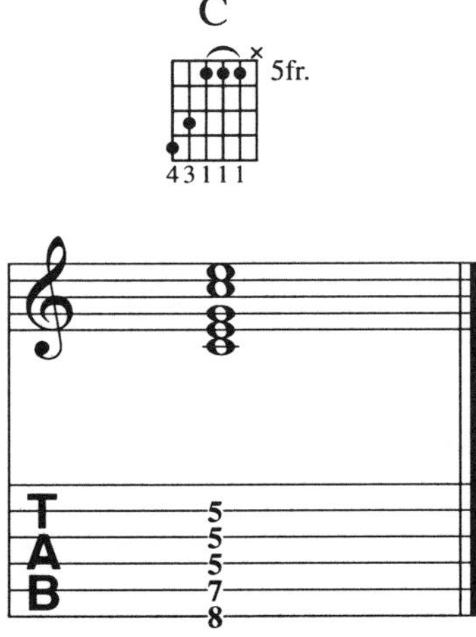

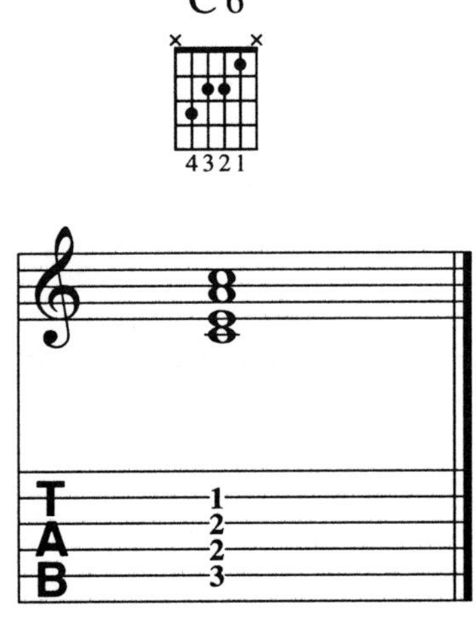

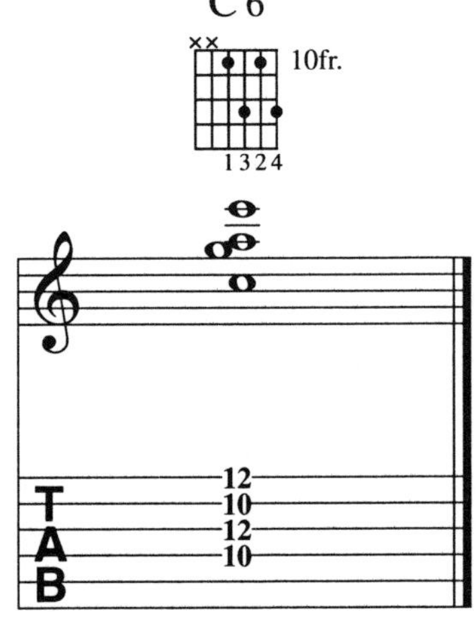

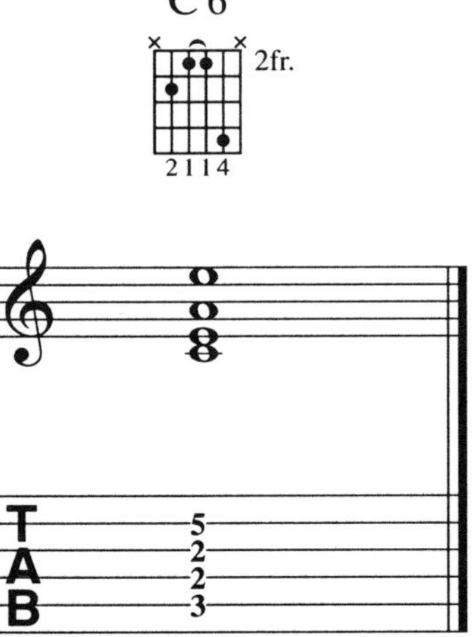

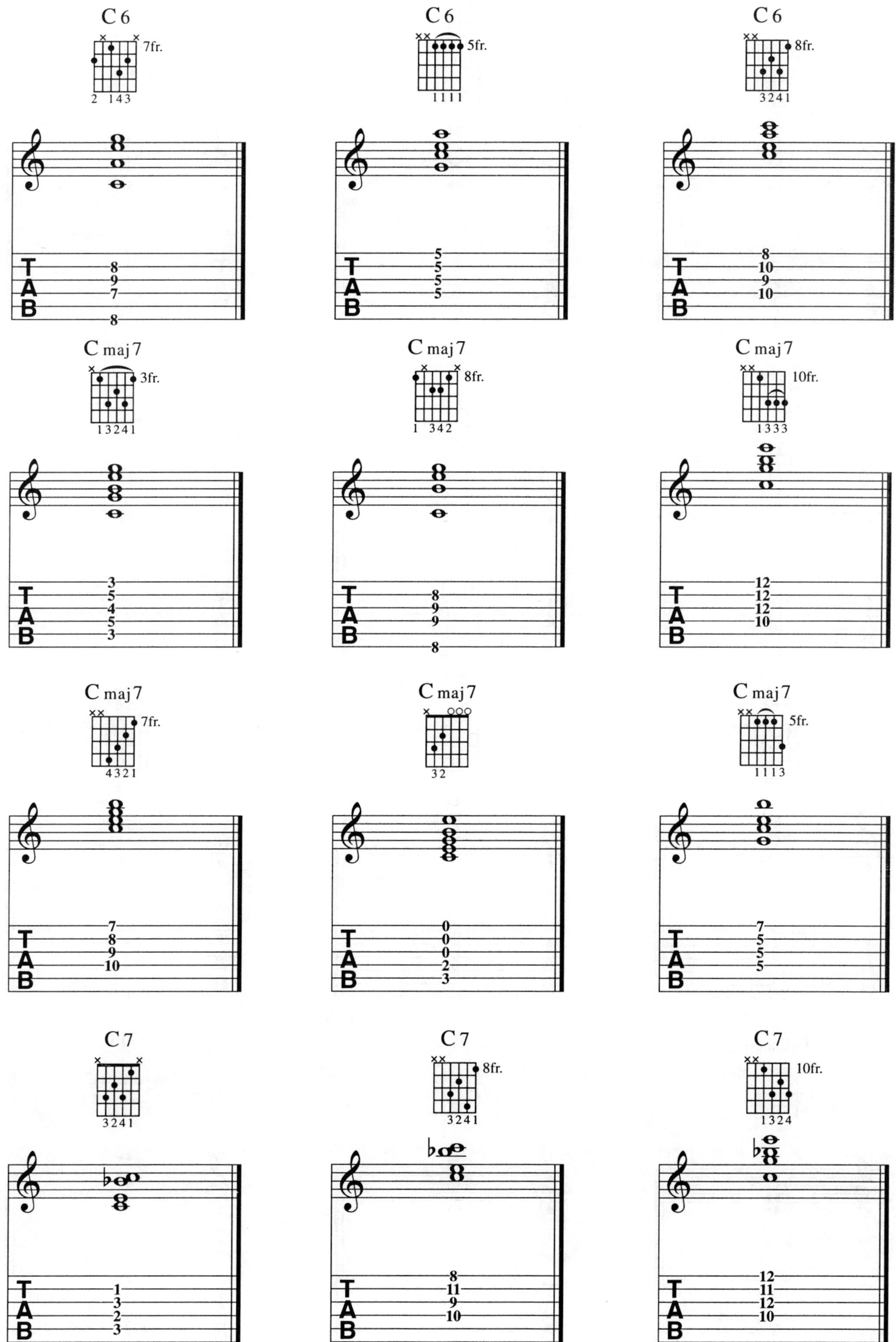

C6
7fr.
2 143
8
9
7
8
C6
5fr.
1111
5
5
5
5
C6
8fr.
3241
8
10
9
10
C maj7
3fr.
13241
3
5
4
5
3
C maj7
8fr.
1 342
8
9
9
8
C maj7
10fr.
1333
12
12
12
10
C maj7
7fr.
4321
7
8
9
10
C maj7
32
0
0
0
2
3
C maj7
5fr.
1113
7
5
5
5
C7
3241
1
3
2
3
C7
8fr.
3241
8
11
9
10
C7
10fr.
1324
12
11
12
10

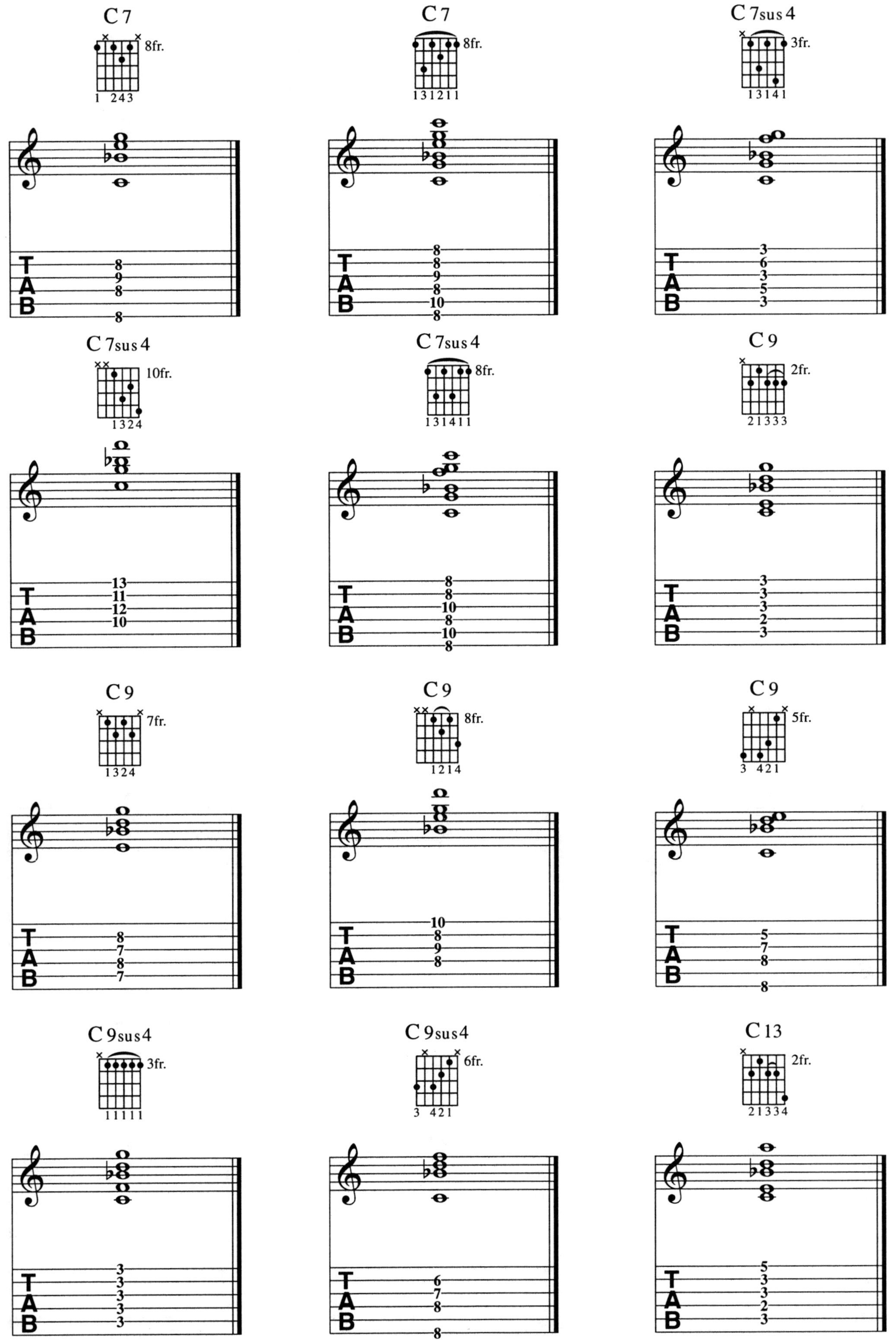
C7
8fr.
1 243
C7
8fr.
131211
C7sus4
3fr.
13141
C7sus4
10fr.
1324
C7sus4
8fr.
131411
C9
2fr.
21333
C9
7fr.
1324
C9
8fr.
1214
C9
5fr.
3 421
C9sus4
3fr.
11111
C9sus4
6fr.
3 421
C13
2fr.
21334

C 13
13fr.
1342
T
A
B
13
14
14
13
C 13
8fr.
1233
10
10
9
8
C 13
8fr.
1 2344
10
10
9
8
8
C 7♯9
2fr.
2134
4
3
2
3
C 7♭9
2fr.
2131
2
3
2
3
C m7♭5
10fr.
1222
11
11
11
10
C m7♭5
3fr.
1324
4
3
4
3
C m7♭5
1342
2
4
3
1
C m7♭5
7fr.
2 341
7
8
8
8
C m
4fr.
231
4
5
5
C m
8fr.
3111
8
8
8
10
C m
11fr.
241
11
13
12

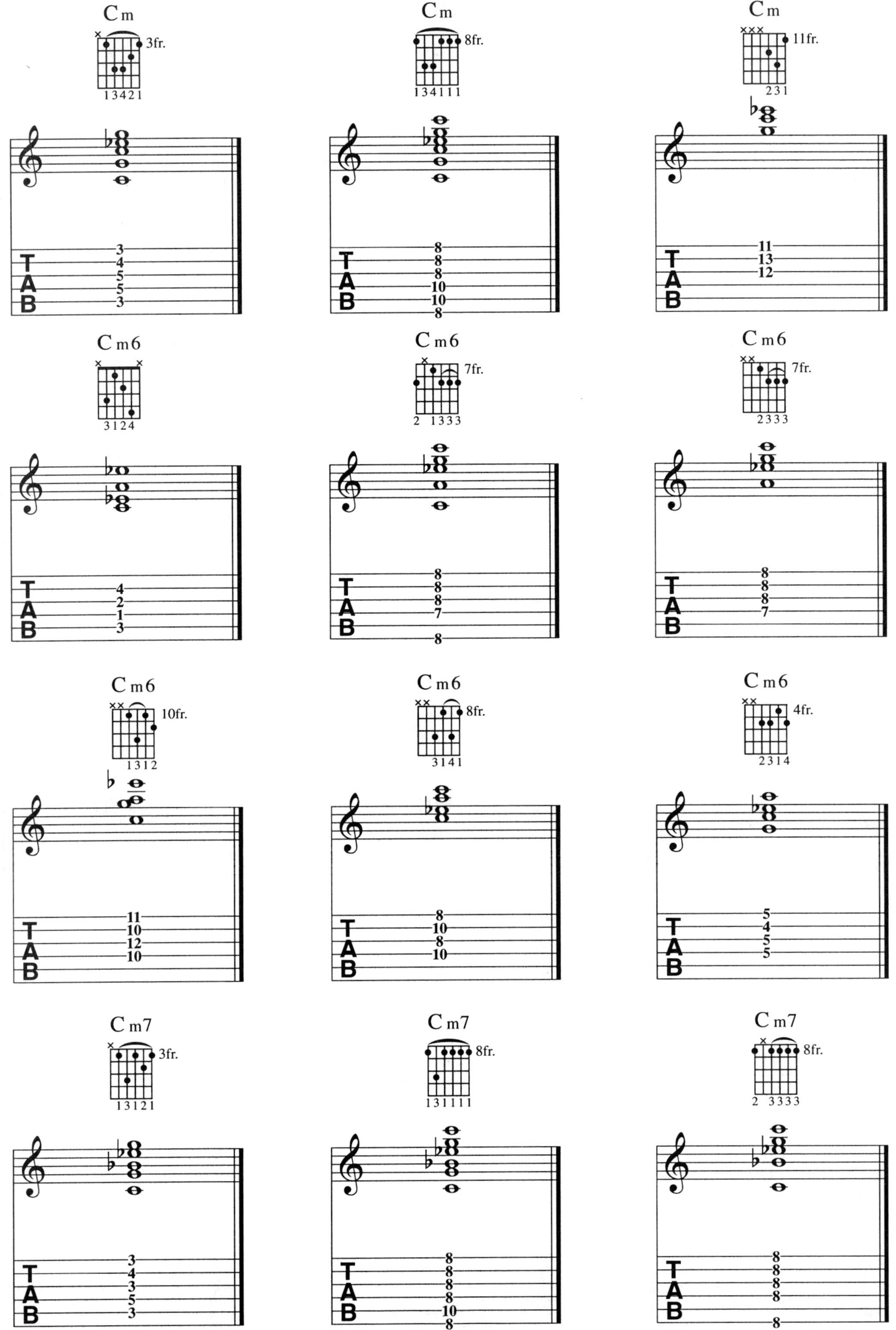
Cm
3fr.
13421
T
A
B
3 4 5 5 3
Cm
8fr.
134111
T
A
B
8 8 8 10 10 8
Cm
11fr.
231
T
A
B
11 13 12
Cm6
3124
T
A
B
4 2 1 3
Cm6
7fr.
2 1333
T
A
B
8 8 8 7 8
Cm6
7fr.
2333
T
A
B
8 8 8 7
Cm6
10fr.
1312
T
A
B
11 10 12 10
Cm6
8fr.
3141
T
A
B
8 10 8 10
Cm6
4fr.
2314
T
A
B
5 4 5 5
Cm7
3fr.
13121
T
A
B
3 4 3 5 3
Cm7
8fr.
131111
T
A
B
8 8 8 8 10 8
Cm7
8fr.
2 3333
T
A
B
8 8 8 8 8

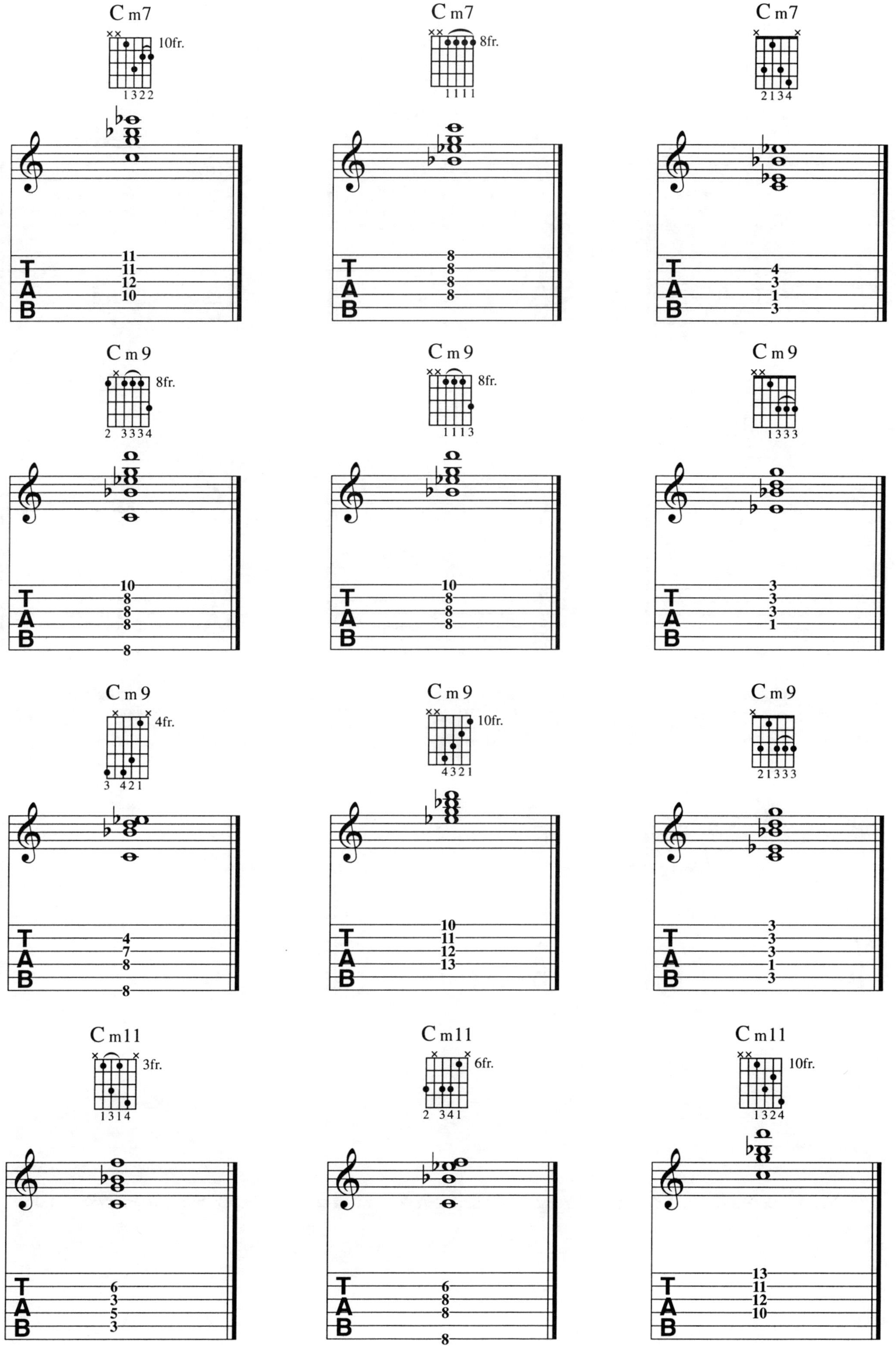
Cm7
10fr.
1322
11
11
12
10
Cm7
8fr.
1111
8
8
8
8
Cm7
2134
4
3
1
3
Cm9
8fr.
2 3334
10
8
8
8
8
Cm9
8fr.
1113
10
8
8
8
Cm9
1333
3
3
3
1
Cm9
4fr.
3 421
4
7
8
8
Cm9
10fr.
4321
10
11
12
13
Cm9
21333
3
3
3
1
3
Cm11
3fr.
1314
6
3
5
3
Cm11
6fr.
2 341
6
8
8
8
Cm11
10fr.
1324
13
11
12
10

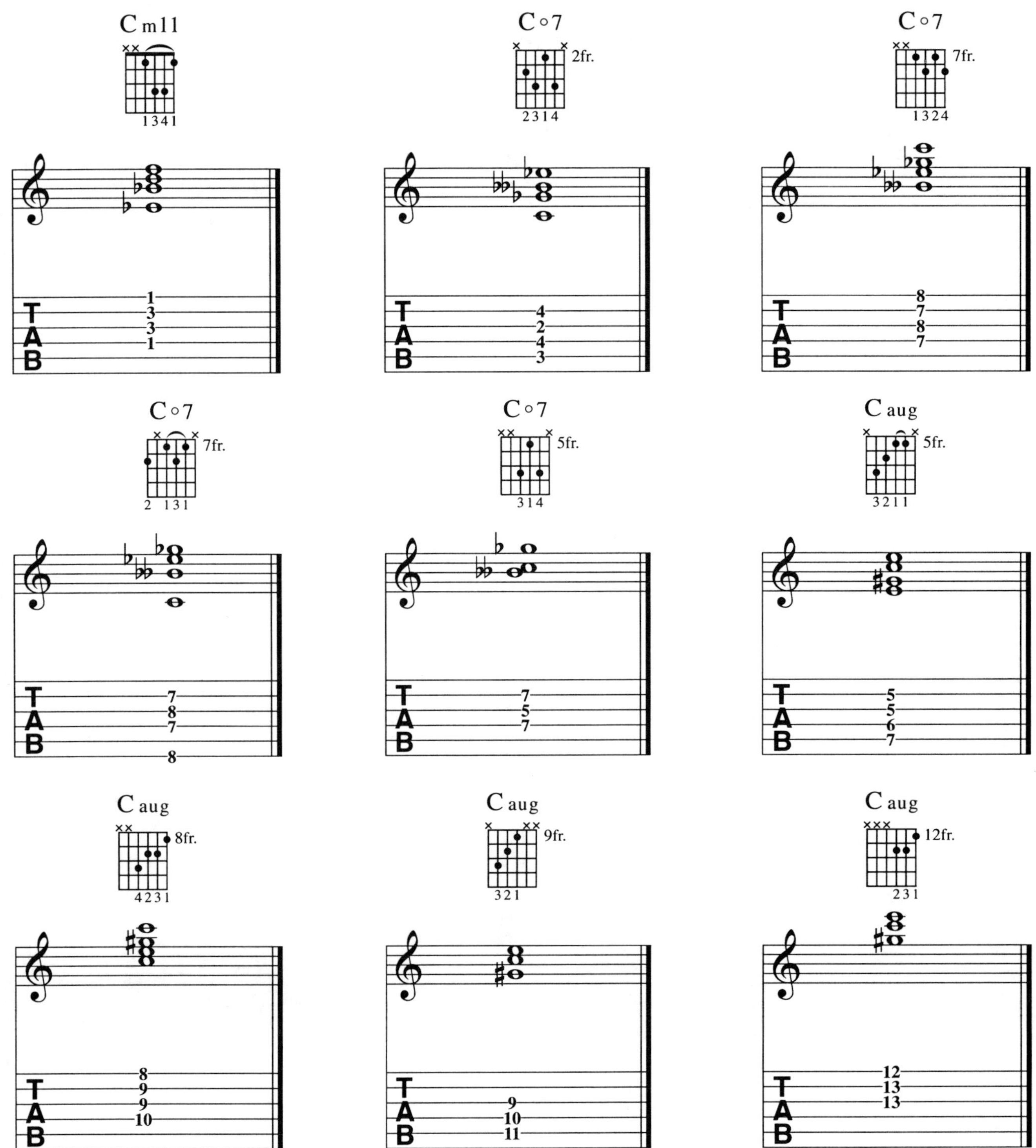
C m11
1341
C∘7
2fr.
2314
C∘7
7fr.
1324
C∘7
7fr.
2 131
C∘7
5fr.
314
C aug
5fr.
3211
C aug
8fr.
4231
C aug
9fr.
321
C aug
12fr.
231
T
A
B

☆☆

Ronald Muldrow

Ronald heard Wes Montgomery playing "Canadian Sunset on the radio while recovering from a broken leg. He was determined to follow in his footsteps of this genius. Subsequent influences on guitar include Kenny Burrell, Grant Green, Phillip Upchurch, Roland Faulkner and George Benson. Muldrow has toured with Eddie Harris, Staple Singers, Lou Rawls, Ronnie Laws, Booker T.Jones and Maceo Parker, to name a few. After a long association with the great, Eddie Harris Ronald moved to New York City where he met Kevin Eubanks. He sometimes subbed for Kevin on gigs; one such memorable occasion was with Roy Haynes' band. Since that time Muldrow has gone on to tour with his own band. Most notably at the Playboy Jazz Festival in Pasadena, CA, and the Newport Jazz Festival in Saratoga, New York. Ronald has received his B.M. in Jazz Studies from Roosevelt University and M.M in Studio/Jazz Guitar from USC. Ronald has released six CD's that have all received recognition in jazz circles. His first CD, "Gnowing You" included such talents as Larry Goldings on organ. Followed by "Yesterdays" featuring the legendary Melvin Rhyne, the original organist with the Wes Montgomery trio. His next CD, "Diaspora",brought Muldrow together with pianist Mulgrew Miller, bassist Peter Washington and drummer Yoron Israel. His fourth CD "Facing Wes" featured vibraphonist Steve Nelson, pianist James Williams, Yoron Israel, Peter Washington. "Freedom's Serenade" features vibraphonist Miller Pertum, pianist Mulgrew Miller, bassist Peter Washington, drummers Yoron Israel and Lorca Hart. Ronald's current release "Mapenzi" along with vibraphonist Miller Pertum, pianists Mulgrew Miller, Donald Vega, bassists Robert Hurst, Peter Washington, drummers Yoron Israel and Lorca Hart. Ronald has also been nominated for best jazz artist (2003) by the LA Black Music Awards.

Visit Ronald Muldrow's website @www.ronaldmuldrow.com

EXCELLENCE IN MUSIC
MEL BAY®
Since 1947